The Journey to

Te[illegible] Figures

A Guide for the
Dark Horse Entrepreneur

JUSTIN BAYLESS

Hardcover: 979-8-9900310-0-5
Paperback: 979-8-9900310-1-2
E-book: 979-8-9900310-2-9

To my family for their generational sacrifices through blood, sweat, and tears.

And to my young family for our relentless Jurni and our everlasting pursuit of Justice and Joy.

Keep Going!!

CONTENTS

FOREWORD

In *The Journey to Ten Figures: A Guide for the Dark Horse Entrepreneur*, Justin Bayless recounts what he considers to be his "unlikely" journey to entrepreneurship. Now, if you have known Justin for any length of time, it doesn't take long to surmise that this man was predestined, even preordained, to be a CEO and a great leader. He is super smart, willing to invest the time to learn and perfect anything, a natural relationship builder, and crucially, he does not like to lose.

You don't have to meet Justin to discover this. His personality and qualities are on clear display here. In this book, Justin presents himself as a determined, "no matter what" young man who evolves into a measured, thoughtful leader who has learned from others how to leverage each experience he has to be better and better. He is inspired, then later challenged, and ultimately motivated by his father to be the best leader that he can be. He delivers an important message to readers that you can be motivated by a great leader, but you do not have to be just like them. You can learn from the great things that they do, learn from their fears, and learn from their mistakes—all valuable lessons—and you can simultaneously be authentically who YOU are.

Such a lesson is important for any leader to learn, but this book will be particularly useful for young leaders who may not even necessarily see themselves as leaders yet. These young people may feel they lack a playbook or an understanding of how to get started, let alone a sense of whether or not they have what it takes to lead themselves, lead others, or be successful. Justin very clearly states in his introduction that this book is for emerging leaders who come by this uncertainty through their personal experiences. Often, they come from communities and surroundings where the prevailing, consistent message that is directly and indirectly given to them is "This is not for you," "You aren't good enough," or "You don't belong here."

It is clear in Justin's recount of his grade school through high school experiences how many times he was told or made to feel that he just didn't measure up—thus the "dark horse" reference in his title and in the book. Simply sharing that experience can offer young leaders proof that such comments are not determinative. However, there is more to the book than just that. Justin also delivers a detailed play-by-play account of how he was challenged to leave what was shaping up to be a successful Wall Street career with a clear playbook, outstanding compensation, and the promise of increasing remuneration, for an offer from his father that was at a 40 percent discount on his income and an unclear path as to exactly what the payoff might be for taking such a risk. Some might have played it easy after taking on that level of risk, but Justin recounts how he aspired to change the entire Arizona system of healthcare to be more efficient and equitable for others when no one had EVER tried such a thing—and no one who looked like him had even dared to consider such an endeavor, not even his father.

He clearly sends a message that as a young leader, one can take on anything—even an entrenched, established system as big as Medicaid—and win through a combination of intelligence, strong relationships, strategic thinking, and perseverance. He underscores the importance of family, being true to oneself, and identifying and honoring what is truly important. These are not easy lessons for any young professional, but Justin shows how, with the right ideas and the people behind you, the seemingly impossible can become possible.

That is what ultimately makes this such a powerful book for young leaders. For those who lack a playbook, Justin provides one of sorts here. The lessons that he has acquired so far in his journey will be a value add for anyone who has made the decision to embark upon the entrepreneurship journey and for anyone who is trying to assess if the journey is for them. *The Journey to Ten Figures* is not only a great, inspiring read, it is a practical tool kit for being a successful entrepreneur and leader.

—Carla Harris, author of *Lead to Win* (2022),
Strategize to Win (2014), and *Expect to Win* (2009)

INTRODUCTION

On May 30, 2008, I handed in my resignation at Morgan Stanley, one of the biggest investment banks in the world. At the time, I was on track for what I believed would be a lucrative career on Wall Street. However, I decided to take a different path: a path not usually so clear to people like me. I was going into ambitious, visionary entrepreneurship.

On that fateful day, I sent an email to my colleagues, family, and friends. In it, I stated my case for leaving in terms of history. I'm a Black man, and the history of my family and my community is one in which opportunities have been systematically denied.

In my email, I recalled the often-forgotten history of Black Wall Street, the business district of Tulsa, Oklahoma, that in 1921 was bombed and burned to the ground by the White community. I sent my email the day before the eighty-seventh anniversary of that event.

But while I found the Black Wall Street Massacre horrifying and enraging, I also found—and still find—a story of aspiration there as well. As I said at the time:

> *The best description of Black Wall Street, or "Little Africa" as it was also known, would be to compare it to a mini–Beverly Hills. It was the golden door of the Black community during the early 1900s, and it proved that African Americans*

could create a successful infrastructure. That's what Black Wall Street was all about.

The dollar circulated thirty-six to one hundred times, sometimes taking a year for currency to leave the community. Now, a dollar leaves the Black community in fifteen minutes. As far as resources, there were PhDs residing in Little Africa, Black attorneys, and doctors. One doctor was Dr. Berry, who owned the bus system. His average income was $500 a day, a hefty pocket change in 1910.

It was a time when the entire state of Oklahoma had only two airports, yet six Blacks owned their own planes. It was a very fascinating community. The mainstay of the community was to educate every child.

You see, Black Wall Street was a beacon on the hill, an example I could follow. I'd grown up in a society that said people from my community only ever saw success through two possible routes: professional degrees with professional jobs working for someone else or through some form of athletics, entertainment, or celebrity.

Sure, a Black man or woman could open their own shop, but ambitious entrepreneurship on the scale I was interested in—the multimillion-dollar or even billion-dollar enterprise—was simply not on the table.

Or at least that was what my peers and I thought at the time.

Black Wall Street offered an inheritance that suggested otherwise. As I said in my email:

While the opportunity to grow and develop under the corporate umbrella presents a premier and tremendous opportunity for most young Black college graduates, many

> *become comfortable and remain idle within the construct for their entire career.*
>
> *When do we completely change this mold? When do we all say it is enough and begin to grow our own businesses for our communities? When is it our time to each branch out and do our own Obama and completely turn the world upside down?*

I ended my letter by saying that I wasn't going to be on the sidelines. I was going back to my home in Arizona to help my father take his small mental health business and change how people practiced mental healthcare across my state.

"History always repeats itself," I wrote. "When the 'Black Wall Street' returns, my question is simple: Are you one who plans to be instrumental in the change or are you one who is simply observant to the change?"

My colleagues, family, and friends had my answer. And with that email sent, I set off to change the world.

Creating Your Own History

When I wrote that email, the overwhelming response from my friends and colleagues was doubt—and some laughter. Someone who looked like me, someone with my background, they didn't scale massive businesses. Who did I think I was, anyway?

I've spent my career proving those doubters wrong. That's been my journey—the journey we'll follow in this book—but this book is not just for young Black people eager to create a similar story for themselves. This is a book for anyone who wants to use entrepreneurship to make a big, positive impact on their community and on the world but who comes from a place where the path to get there is at best obscure and often appears closed.

This is a book for the people who wake up and know they are supposed to be doing *something big* with their lives but who find themselves following the traditional paths others expect them to walk. It's for those who feel *stuck* because they have obligations to their family, because they are in debt, or especially, because they come from a community where there are no examples of entrepreneurial success on a large scale. For those who grew up without a playbook, without a road map, and without a mentor in their community to show the way, this book is for you.

It's for anyone who wants to break free of the trends of history and create their own history. And it's for those who are willing to invest themselves completely in that project.

This is a standard I have always held myself to. On the wall at my company, I had two posters. The first was a famous quote from Apple's "Think Different" campaign:

> Here's to the crazy ones, the misfits, the rebels, the troublemakers, the round pegs in the square holes, the ones who see things differently. They're not fond of rules, and they have no respect for the status quo. You can quote them, disagree with them, glorify or vilify them. About the only thing you can't do is ignore them . . . Because the ones who are crazy enough to think they can change the world are the ones who do.

The second was a picture of two hands—those of Morpheus from *The Matrix*. In each hand, there was a pill—the red and the blue. That posture demanded that I make the choice every day between the well-trod path and the one I was blazing.

Those two posters were not on my wall simply as a matter of taste (although I do love *The Matrix*). They spoke to what it takes for someone to change the world when they have the odds stacked against them. It requires vision, determination, and a willingness to buy in and commit 100 percent.

I know the next generation has what it takes. In fact, I'm betting on it. The reason I'm writing this book is to reach out to the next generation of "dark horse" entrepreneurs who will beat the odds and lead their companies to unicorn status: hitting a billion-dollar valuation as a private company.

A dark horse is anyone that the rest of the world dismisses, the major player that seems to come out of nowhere. That's the sort of entrepreneur I've been my whole career, and it's the sort I want to help raise up—now that the opportunities to transform dark horses into unicorns are finally more available.

A New Era with New Opportunities . . . for All

For centuries, the opportunities to really change the world were heavily guarded. Often, it was only White, rich men with the right connections who could take their shot at transformational business. Those who dared to try to push their way in were kicked out—often with brutal force. The Black Wall Street Massacre is the most vicious example of this, but it certainly isn't the only one. Women, communities of every color, and really any community below the "elite" have an infinite number of stories that follow a similar pattern.

But we live in a time when *more* is becoming possible for many of us. Traditionally, for a business to reach the height of growth and influence, it had to solve issues of scalability and investment. General Motors, IBM, Walmart, Coca-Cola: these companies had to be able to grow physically, and that required access and funds from the gatekeepers—a good old boy network of investment firms and venture capitalists.

Those barriers have begun to fall. There are now new ways to access opportunity—ways no one can guard. Technology has reduced the pressure to scale across physical locations. Consider just how much opportunity one company, Shopify, has created. It has opened the doors to thousands of entrepreneurs from every background to create their own web platforms and run their own e-commerce businesses. Odds are that the next billionaire entrepreneur will grow via a virtual enterprise instead of through expensive physical infrastructure. We've already seen the likes of Mark Zuckerberg and Marc Benioff change the world. As I write this book, we're seeing it happen again with Sam Altman at OpenAI. And this isn't exclusively seen at these world-conquering companies. Shadiah Sigala is a first-generation Mexican immigrant and a cofounder of the $2 billion HoneyBook. Iman Abuzeid cofounded Incredible Health that helps nurses find new roles. She's raised tens of millions in funding for her company. Toyin Ajayi is another cofounder in the health sphere, creating Cityblock Health with Iyah Romm that is trying to increase access to holistic healthcare—an aim close to my own heart.

The list goes on. I have no crystal ball and can't guarantee all of these entrepreneurs will maintain their success, but the pattern is clear. The opportunities for this kind of success are there—and they are available to everyone.

We are living in an era of disruptive technological opportunity. Thanks to Moore's Law—which states the power of micro-technology will continually double as the price halves—we will see incredible potential for explosive growth across almost every industry over the coming decades. Within our lifetimes, we'll see the death of the combustion engine, the rise of artificial intelligence solutions, and untold changes in energy, currency, and the ways we connect. And all it takes to access the potential within this change is a computer.

I have volunteered at the Boys & Girls Club of the Valley, and I have taught entrepreneurship to high school students. I tell all these budding entrepreneurs that everyone in the room could be a millionaire within a year. I'm not misleading them. That's how much potential technology is unlocking for us every day.

That's not to say you have to become an expert coder or become an engineer to create a business that can change the world. I helped change an entire state's Medicaid system, and I'm not a doctor.

The point is that opportunity is there for you—if you're willing to take it. It's more complicated than that, of course. To really make that kind of change takes incredible fortitude to push through remaining barriers. It requires absorbing the lessons life is teaching you, developing your skills in entrepreneurship, and relying on the wisdom of those around you. It requires embracing the journey—with all its twists and turns, mountains and valleys, triumphs and setbacks. But the opportunity is there.

It's there partly because of a second major change that is reducing barriers. Traditional funding vehicles are proliferating. Twenty years ago, the primary source of early-stage capital was venture capital funding. Today, the process is opening up, with online platforms offering new alternatives. In addition, more women and people of color are getting into the rooms where decisions are made, and that means more opportunity is opening up for those who have been locked out of entrepreneurship to finally get a fair hearing.

Whether you come from an underrepresented and marginalized community or simply don't have people in your life who encourage entrepreneurship, the opportunity is there. It can be difficult to see a path to realizing it, but if you have the ambition and the dream, you can find a way forward.

That's what I hope to give you by sharing my story. This is a book about how I did it. I faced discrimination, doubt, and hard times. I had to chase down investments and convince a state's medical bureaucracy to take my ideas seriously. I found a way through it all. As we navigate how I did it, I'll share some of the key lessons I learned: lessons that I hope push you forward where I stumbled and allow you to rise even higher than I did.

Taking the Dark Horse Path

When I left Morgan Stanley, almost no one thought it was a good idea. I had two very clear paths to success in front of me. I could keep working on Wall Street, or I could try to go to work in the sports and entertainment industry with my brother, Jerryd, who was about to be drafted into the NBA.

There before me were the traditional paths for those that society has held back. I could work under someone else in a good profession, or I could piggyback on my brother's basketball career.

When I chose entrepreneurship, I was very much a dark horse. No one expected me to have the level of entrepreneurial success that I accomplished. In fact, no one even saw the vision. For years, no one believed I could turn my father's small mental health business into any sort of success. When I met friends in the community or at home, they didn't even ask about my company. They wanted to know about my brother. They wanted to know where he was playing and how his career was going.

Even to them, I was the "other brother"—the one who had made a bizarre choice to walk away from the straightforward path to success. I won't lie. That really annoyed me. And it motivated me to prove them all wrong.

That's just what I did. My vision—once so derided everyone ignored it in conversation—proved transformative. I took on the Arizona Medicaid system and changed it. I grew immense value in the company, helped thousands of people, and provided greater care for the entire state. When I sold that little mom-and-pop company, it had a nine-figure valuation and was a national leader in both integrated care and telemedicine.

Now, I want to empower entrepreneurs like you to grow without sacrificing your values and to receive guidance and funding from nontraditional sources—ones that welcome you instead of keeping you out. Eventually, I hope to help one of you to reach a ten-figure valuation for your company.

Like Bill Russell, I've entered a new era of my career as a "player–coach." I'm still in the game, still driving to win titles myself, but I'm also looking to lift others up to become champions.

That's where we'll end up. But before we get to your future, we have to first talk about my past.

I

BAYLIS AND BAYLESS

My story has to begin with my parents. Not only did they play the biggest part in forming my personality, they—along with my extended family—provided me with my foundational understanding of business and the hustle it takes for success.

This is most obvious in the story of my father, Michael B. Bayless, known to anyone close to him as Brad. My father was a very well-known man. The company at the heart of this story still has his last name on it—my last name. Through my father, I met athletes and the brothers of presidential candidates, as we shall soon see. He spent time with governors and FBI agents. His reputation continues to flourish in the years since his death.

On a more personal note, he was also my best friend and my greatest mentor. Needless to say, he will play a huge role in all that follows in this book.

For all these reasons, though, I would rather start this book talking not about him but about my mother. Mom never founded her own company (though she was instrumental in the establishment of my father's business). She didn't have meetings with prominent politicians or work with a professional sports team. She didn't go golfing with high-level executives. All the same, I am confident that I could never have achieved success on the journey ahead without her.

She was instrumental in raising me with the values that led to my success. She cultivated my nascent entrepreneurial instincts and pushed me to excel.

It's only fitting, then, that I start a book about the less obvious paths to success by discussing my "dark horse parent," whose role was no less crucial for its less traditional form of success.

Mom's Family

Denise Bowman, or Mom to me, was born in 1958. She was the daughter of Fred Bowman of Saginaw, Michigan—a tough military man who was the first Black first lieutenant in postwar Germany—and Vera Schwarz, a White German woman he met while stationed over there. In very postwar Germany fashion, Fred and Vera met in a nightclub. At the time, it was common for pretty young German women to date young American soldiers. Vera had learned enough English from school to be able to communicate, and they hit it off. In fact, they quickly fell in love.

Denise Bowman (Mom)

A year into their relationship, they decided to get married, and that's when they first ran into trouble. The army had rules against interracial marriage. But my grandfather is a determined and insistent man—a trait that very much runs in the family—and he somehow got his way.

Perhaps that first success misled him. Perhaps he thought determination was enough to overcome all the obstacles the world had set before him. He must have thought something along those lines because when he and Vera found out Mom was on the way, they headed back to the States.

Grandad, as I have always known him, wanted to be sure my mother was born a U.S. citizen—he wasn't aware she would be one anyway because of his citizenship—and I suppose he assumed that the power and privilege he experienced as a U.S. officer in Germany would follow him back to America. He was wrong. Nineteen fifty-eight America was not a friendly place for a young Black man, particularly one with a White wife.

Mom's Childhood

Mom was born in Michigan. Her home in Detroit was on a street named Baylis—a name that would, in time, have great significance for her, although spelled differently. Her earliest years saw the complete dissolution of her parents' marriage. Fred and Vera had very little in common. That, combined with the tensions that came from raising Mom, my aunt Monique, and my uncle Fred and the racism they experienced as a mixed-race couple in America, led to their divorce when Mom was just four years old.

With the divorce, Vera walked away from her role as a mother for the most part. When Grandad pushed for full custody, she didn't put up much of a fight. She moved to New York and later Florida and pursued a modeling career.

After the divorce, Vera's mother, Frieda, came from Germany to take care of the kids while my grandfather worked. He found it difficult to make ends meet with three kids and no other support raising them. His parents helped out as much as they could, but they had twenty grandchildren, leaving them with only so much time to help Grandad's kids.

Later, when Mom was in fourth grade, she and her siblings went with Frieda back to Germany for eighteen months while Grandpa Bowman worked and saved money. It was an experience she would never forget.

Berlin was such a cosmopolitan city. At twice the population of Detroit and far freer for a young Black girl, it felt so much bigger than anything she'd previously experienced. Mom knew then that she wanted a life beyond what Detroit could offer her. That ambition for something more would remain with her for the rest of her life.

Meanwhile, Grandad was working his way up from loading buses at Greyhound to becoming one of the company's first Black executives. When Mom and her siblings came back to Detroit, they found their father was working in Chicago. One weekend, he brought a woman named Wilda home and introduced her to the kids. A month later, they announced they were getting married. A few months after that, without any further meetings between Wilda and the kids, Grandad and Wilda tied the knot, and shortly thereafter moved the whole family to Shaker Heights, Ohio, a small town outside of Cleveland.

What followed was the worst five years of my mother's life. From the freedom and seemingly unlimited potential of Berlin, she found herself pulled away from the support structures that she had known all her life—the aunts, uncles, cousins, grandparents, and friends that she relied on. In their place was a woman she didn't know at all; a woman she struggled to bond with. Wilda must also have been feeling lost and overwhelmed by the dramatic shift in her life. After all, she left Chicago as suddenly as my mom left Detroit. Everyone's lives were disrupted by that relocation, and they were all left to deal with the changes as best they could.

Facing an unhappy home life, Mom chose to turn her attention toward escape. Throughout that period, she became increasingly driven and self-reliant. She excelled in school and was skipped two grades, allowing her to graduate high school at sixteen. She started spending time with her boyfriend's family, where she got to know what it was like in a Black household with college-educated parents. So when Grandad prepared to uproot the family again—this time moving them to Arizona—she told him she wasn't going.

On her own at only sixteen, Mom got an apartment, and within three years, she had bought her own house. She started out working in retail for Horten's Dairy. After a year, she was so successful, the company promoted her to sales manager and moved her to Detroit where she could represent them with the 7-Eleven stores in that area. She paid all her bills without any assistance. But eventually, after six years on her own, Mom decided she wanted more. It was time for a new challenge. She planned to go out to California. Along the way, she stopped off in Arizona. Then she met Dad, and her plans changed.

A Man of Firsts

My father's beginnings were very different from my mom's. Mom came from a family that had seen the world. Dad grew up in the town of Portsmouth, Ohio—a place that felt like no one could ever get out.

Mom was the child of a mixed-race couple. When Dad was born in 1948, Portsmouth was still segregated. The city lay on the north side of the Ohio River, across the border from Kentucky. His father—Walter, although everyone called him Buddy—was a product of that location. He had served in World War II, but his future would be very different from Fred Bowman's. He was ambitious in his way, but there were limited options for a Black man in a segregated town. For a time, he owned a dump truck. He was also part owner of a restaurant. His main enterprise, though, was number running, an illegal gambling operation. All in all, he was what you might call a hustler—always willing to try something and take any opportunity. Unfortunately, it eventually caught up with him. Because of his number running, he got in trouble with the law and had to flee the state.

By that time, he and my grandmother, Julia Bell, had split up. Raising Dad and his brother, Shannon, largely on her own, she was a truly impressive woman. She was a nurse and an entrepreneur. She owned her own beauty shop—in fact, the only Black beauty shop in town. She also owned the building next to it, where she ran the only Black club. And she owned her own home. Despite society being against her, she achieved incredible things. It's not hard to see where Dad's drive came from.

Buddy and Julia Bell did the best they could for Dad. They were good parents living in tough circumstances. Where they fell short, Dad could rely on the wider Portsmouth community. The neighborhood was close and very supportive of one another. They lived the "it takes a village" mentality to heart. That belief in raising up your community along with yourself would stick with Dad, and he would pass it down to the next generation.

Dad became particularly close with his mother's family, the Tubbs. Growing up, his Grandma Nancy and Grandpa Tubbs were like a second set of parents, and his first cousins—Ila, Dennis, and Stephanie—were more like siblings. They were all to a person smart and ambitious like him, though they, like everyone else in Portsmouth, were surprised when Dad decided to head across the country to become the first in the family to go to college.

The younger generation all had the goal of getting out of Portsmouth, but for most of them, their ticket was the military. This was the height of Vietnam, and the general consensus was it was better to sign up and choose to serve in the Air Force than get drafted and have to fight in the jungle. Fortuitously, Dad broke his foot and couldn't serve, so he headed out to Arizona—where his dad had ended up after running from the law.

The whole family stayed close, even as they spread across the country to find their own ways to success. Ila would go on to found an enormous nurse staffing organization in Atlanta, and Stephanie would eventually become a congresswoman. Dad was always very involved in their lives. When Dennis went through chemo, Dad was right there with him, supporting him. After Stephanie died in a car crash after suffering an aneurysm while driving, it was the most upset I ever saw my father. It was one of only two times I ever saw the man cry.

Cousin Stephanie with Dad

Out in Arizona, Dad thrived. He loved being a leader, and he was a man who was unafraid to be first. While on a scholarship at Northern Arizona University (NAU), he helped charter Epsilon Upsilon, the local chapter of the Kappa Alpha Psi fraternity. Founded in 1911, Kappa Alpha Psi is a historically majority African American fraternity with chapters across the country. I still have the photo of Dad in 1969, huge afro on his head, smiling at the founding ceremony.

After graduating from NAU, Dad pushed even more boundaries. He went on to get his master's and doctorate in counseling psychology at Arizona State University (ASU). It was there that the psychologists he trained under saw promise in him and encouraged him to work in forensic psychology—the practice that would make his name.

From 1977 to 1981, he honed those skills. Then the FBI contacted him to be their expert forensic psychology witness in the Wayne Williams trial. Dad was the first Black forensic psychologist working with the FBI, and that case was national news. The book and show *Mindhunter* on Netflix culminate in the trial that Dad featured in.

After the case, Dad's reputation attracted the attention of the Arizona government and Department of Health Services. The state reached out to him to open a Medicaid mental health clinic for children in inner-city Phoenix with the aim of addressing the needs of minority communities that were otherwise severely underserved.

In 1982, he incorporated his practice under the name Michael B. Bayless & Associates, P.C. To open the business, he sought a loan from the most unexpected of sources: the Goldwater family. For those of you who don't know, Barry Goldwater was the 1964 Republican nominee for president. He was, to put it mildly, very conservative.

Yet such was Dad's magnetic personality—and such was the openness of Barry's brother Bob—that the Goldwater family provided the loan that allowed Bayless & Associates to open its doors with a simple handshake.

That was just one of Dad's talents. He could talk to anyone, and he could find a connection even when there were enormous differences between himself and his conversation partner. He had the vision, the passion, and the talent to convince anyone to trust where he was taking them.

Business and Family

In 1981, along with the success he found in his career, Dad hit the jackpot a second time when he met Mom. Perhaps it was all going to his head. According to my mother, her first thought when he introduced himself was that he was "pretty obnoxious." He interrupted her date with another man to give her his card. Yet, as he so often did, he left an impression. When she saw him two weeks later, she decided to pay him back and crashed his date. To her surprise, though, he simply left the other woman he'd been sitting with and spent the afternoon with her.

On their first official date a week later, Dad clearly knew where he wanted this relationship to go. He asked her what she thought their kids would look like.

She thought he was crazy. He wasn't. A year later, they were married—the same year Bayless & Associates opened its doors.

Together, they turned Bayless & Associates into a real company. At the time, Dad had a second business focused on digitizing psychological assessments. As that fell through, Mom encouraged him to focus his attention on Bayless. In the early months of operations, she ran the front desk and shared her considerable business sense to help get things up and running—a sense Dad mostly lacked.

Two years later, though, everything changed again. That's when I showed up. While Mom continued to keep the books for the company until the time that my parents separated, she mostly left Bayless & Associates behind to focus on being a mother. The gift of time is very important to my mother, and she believed it was of the greatest importance to give as much of it as possible in the first five years of her children's lives. While not every family can afford to have a parent stay home, she knew the value of that role when it was possible. And she was determined to give her children the best shot at success.

That's not to say she settled into a life defined only by raising kids and tending to the house. She kept working and kept seeking ways to raise us up in the world. She trained to be a court reporter, but she walked away a year and a half into her course because she found the work unfulfilling. She later became a real estate agent and began remodeling homes, finding value and beauty in what others discarded. Her greatest work in remodeling, though, was done for the family's benefit.

Years before house flipping was a commonly understood business opportunity, Mom discovered that the fastest way to upgrade the family's social position was by moving us into a house, fixing it up, selling it, and investing the profits in a house in a better neighborhood.

My whole childhood, we were moving to ever-better neighborhoods. Before I was twelve, we'd moved four times. Even though most people believed it was solely due to my father's work, my mother played a key role in our family moving from lower middle-class to upper middle-class. She was an entrepreneur without a business, and our welfare was her primary project.

Part of that project was giving me a sense of business and economics from a young age. Mom taught me about the stock market and encouraged my interest by showing me how to track stocks I cared about. The Boston Celtics and LA Lakers were publicly traded. While Magic and Bird were battling on the court, she helped me keep track of how the team's stock price was doing on the market. She also pointed me toward IBM's stock, since that's where my uncle Fred worked.

Because of her, I started asking for stocks as a birthday gift instead of presents. Because of her, I was learning how to write checks and balance books at financial summer camp by age ten.

Unfortunately, Dad was less focused on developing a business strategy. He was a brilliant psychologist, a wonderful conversationalist, a great dad, and a visionary thinker, but he had never learned how to match business execution to ideas.

His understanding of business principles was rudimentary. He was happy if his Quicken account showed the company in the black at the end of the month. If it was in the red, he was grouchy. He lacked the technical training to handle anything beyond basic business situations, and that meant there was little hope of growing Bayless & Associates into an enterprise under his leadership.

And that was a great shame because Dad was decades ahead of his time in mental health. Way back in the '80s, he was looking for ways to provide mental health services in people's homes. While the rest of the mental health community continued to expect every client to come into the office or forego assistance, Dad knew that the people of his community often lacked the ability or motivation to cross town to visit a therapist.

It was hard for working people to get the time off to go to a therapist, and harder still to arrange transportation. Making matters worse, there was a stigma against therapy in the under-represented minority communities. But if a therapist could come to the people who needed help, it could be done privately and on that person's schedule.

The idea was brilliant, but Dad had no idea how to organize it. No matter how successful he was elsewhere, he couldn't find a way to transfer that success into the inner-city clinic.

In 1986, he started consulting with the Phoenix Suns as a team psychologist because of the substance abuse issues prevalent among the players in the '80s. He later became close friends with Frank Johnson, the team's first Black coach, and Eddie Johnson, the team commentator.

He continued to be a reliable resource for the FBI—as well as county attorneys, defense attorneys, and others—as a forensic psychologist.

The forensic side of his practice grew and brought in revenue. But the Medicaid community-based clinic simply stumbled along—remaining stubbornly small, limited, and unprofitable. And it would remain that way throughout my childhood.

2

RISING PHOENIX

My parents were very different people who didn't often see eye to eye, but they were completely aligned in one area. They believed pushing my brother and I would give us the best future we could possibly have. They envisioned us running faster and working harder than anyone else so that we could create better lives for ourselves.

While Mom was teaching me about stocks and personal finance, Dad stressed performance, performance, performance. Above all, he knew how to put his head down and work incredibly hard. He accrued as many academic achievements and credentials as he could. He knew they might not make him successful, but they would at least give him a chance. Working hard was like breathing for him, in the sense that it was utterly necessary, every moment of every day. And he expected his sons to share this same commitment.

"There's no substitute for excellence" was Dad's golden rule—the principle that governed his life—and that was a rule he expected us to follow as well.

I vividly recall Dad coming home from work early on my first day of first grade in elementary school. I was in my bedroom writing in my notebook.

"How was school?" he asked.

"It was okay." I went back to my notebook.

I don't remember what I was writing, but I know it was the messy, disorganized writing of a child on his first day of first grade. When Dad saw that, he snatched the paper out from under my pencil and ripped it to pieces while I watched, shocked and hurt.

"Go sharpen your pencil," he commanded, "and start again from scratch. We don't do anything that's second best. Whatever you do, it always has to be excellent."

When it came to perfection with work, my dad didn't play.

Young Justin with Dad

Mom's tactics were different, but her perspective was the same. She believed in the old saying, "No one rises to low expectations." But she also believed in nurturing the individual talents of her two sons instead of pushing us toward some general idea of excellence. She wanted us to excel—but in the areas of our natural skills and inclinations.

At an early age, she had Jerryd and I fill out psychological assessments that were reviewed by an independent psychologist to see where our talents lay. While Jerryd was clearly a gifted athlete, my strongest abilities resided elsewhere. And that meant that no matter how much I loved basketball, academics had to come first—hence the stocks and finance classes.

To motivate us, Mom tried to combine a certain strictness with a positive example. Mom didn't believe in corporal punishment—but that doesn't mean she wasn't firm. She expected a lot, and we were expected to live up to our potential. But she also expected a lot of herself. While raising us, she made sure to complete her own college degree that she'd worked on piecemeal since she was sixteen so that I'd have no excuse to avoid college once I finished high school. By the time I graduated, she had a master's degree in counseling from ASU and was part of the counseling faculty at Maricopa Community College.

This shared firmness and ambition from my parents meant that I missed out on some of the fun the other kids seemed to be having. Summers, for instance, involved as much school as play. But it was all in the cause of teaching me a valuable lesson: if you want to be a success in anything, you have to find your talents and possess a relentless drive to achieve it.

Too Black and Too White

In a lot of ways, Dad's focus on excellence and performance aided my concentration on my own internal drive. His parenting helped me develop the discipline I needed to be successful. Mom, on the other hand, turned her eye toward the wider world. And that meant getting into the right places where success could happen.

Even though my dad wasn't convinced of the value of private education, Mom fought him until he agreed to let us apply to one of the top private schools in Phoenix for our primary education. There, Jerryd and I would rub elbows with the smartest and most successful families in Arizona. The courses were also guaranteed to challenge us. Sixth grade at my private school was every inch as difficult as some of my college courses. I attended from kindergarten until sixth grade, and Jerryd, who was five years behind me, from kindergarten to second.

At first, going to school was a positive experience. Though some of my classmates were unbelievably wealthy, people were generally friendly. No one paid a lot of attention to the fact that I was one of the only three Black kids there.

Gradually, that changed.

With every passing year it got tougher to be one of the only kids at my school who looked like me. The other kids started messing with me—touching my hair and calling me names—things like that.

I was a pretty skinny kid of about average size initially, but getting into scuffles and even full-on fights from time to time became more and more common. Oddly enough, some of the kids who became my close friends were initially kids I fought with more than once.

Unfortunately, it wasn't just the other students who made life difficult. When I was in first grade, a teacher separated me from the other students in my classroom and tried to give me remedial work. It didn't seem to matter to her that my grades were good or that I'd never given her any reason to believe I needed material that was easier than everyone else's. In other words, there was no *good* reason she should've lowered her expectations just for me.

That was the kind of treatment Mom wouldn't stand for. When I went home that day and told her what had happened, she flew up to the school, as fierce as I've ever seen her, and demanded to know what was going on and who was going to fix it. She told the teacher that my IQ test results and my evaluations from kindergarten proved I was more than intelligent enough for grade-level material. The teacher backed down, and I was given work that matched my level.

This was not the last time a teacher would single me out for different treatment. My fourth-grade teacher didn't physically separate me or insult my intelligence, but she treated me differently all the same. When my class was learning about civil rights, she decided I—and I alone—should be the one to read everything about Martin Luther King, Jr.

Each of these events subtly formed my future character. In particular, I believe this was the start of the chip that would settle on my shoulder throughout my career. Seeing others look down on me made me determined—even at that young age—to prove them wrong. And that meant failure, or even just mediocrity, was not an option. I was going to prove that I was not just capable, I was more than capable.

Fourth grade was also the year I got really good at basketball—so good, in fact, that I outplayed all the kids my own age and couldn't play on their teams. I started playing with the seventh and eighth graders, but I was better than them too. When the parents of those seventh and eighth graders complained I was taking a spot on the team, my parents had to find another league for me that was competitive enough to challenge me. That's how I was introduced to the Boys & Girls Club.

And I'm so glad I was. The Boys & Girls Club became a safe haven where I could just play basketball and forget everything else going on in my life.

There was a lot I wanted to forget. In particular, there was my parents' marriage that was deteriorating. Their regular arguments began to escalate and become more frequent. Ultimately, they had simply grown to be too different. My mom was ten years younger than my dad—a gap that hadn't mattered that much early on but meant Mom was still learning who she was when they first married. After two kids and many more years of living, she'd changed—and my dad hadn't changed with her. They split up for good when I was in sixth grade. A year before my parents divorced, we moved to the east side of Phoenix, and I transitioned from my private school to a public middle school. Jerryd and I began taking the bus to school and home, alternating between our parents' residences.

The poor treatment I received at the private school was even worse at middle school. It didn't even take two months for a kid to call me the n-word. I got suspended for fighting back. In the following weeks, another kid on the bus put gum in my hair—I was wearing an afro back then—and I fought him right there on the bus. I was suspended for that one too.

What I quickly learned is that Black and White stereotypes are interesting—and alienating—on both sides of the community. In middle school I was an athlete in honors academics who spoke and wrote very well. As I transitioned into a private Catholic high school with more diversity than any other schools I'd attended, I didn't quite fit into any community. I was too Black for the overly White world of academic honors classes and too White for the predominantly Black and Hispanic world of sports. I was respected by the basketball team, but I wasn't cool enough to be one of the guys. The White kids in my classes looked at me a little differently too.

The fact that I didn't fit neatly into any stereotype contributed to the growing sense of isolation I'd felt in some way my whole childhood. Of all the worlds I was part of, none of them were a perfect fit. I struggled to find any place where I felt like I truly belonged. At the time it was painful, but it was good practice for what was ahead. Already, I was pushing against expectations and going my own way. I was already a dark horse at the start of my journey.

The Wrong Neighborhood

Despite those struggles, I still managed to excel. My grades were high, and by my junior year, I'd been made captain of my high school varsity basketball team—one of the best basketball teams in the state. But that didn't protect me from those same societal tensions that had followed me throughout my youth. One day after practice, I was driving home in my green Dodge, music blaring, windows down, the wind blowing through my car. I planned to shower when I got home, so I was still wearing my jersey. At that time, I was about six foot four, and I wore my hair in a gigantic 'fro, styled after a character in a retro basketball video game. I was seventeen, and I wasn't a small kid anymore.

As I reached Camelback Road the urban grit of Phoenix gave way to expansive suburban homes with lots of square footage and precise landscaping. Land that had once been used for orchards now boasted the most expensive homes in the area. Thanks to Mom's gift for real estate, we'd gotten in before things blew up. In a sense, that neighborhood and I grew up together. It was home.

But that evening, home turned out to be nice enough to cause me trouble.

I pulled up to the first of two four-way stops between me and my dad's house that was in the same area. I looked both ways. To my right, I saw a cop car. *Great*, I thought. The police car started tailing me as soon as I entered the intersection. I turned my music down.

I drove toward the second stop, careful to follow the speed limit. After the second stop, I turned left onto my street. I was so close to home at that point that if I'd had a rock in my hand, I could've thrown it and hit my house. That's when the lights started flashing in my rearview.

I pulled over. The officer asked where I was going. He asked for my license, and I had to tell him that I didn't have it. It was in my green Nike gym bag, which was locked in my trunk.

"So," he said, "you don't have any identification?"

"No, sir. But I live right there," I said, pointing at Dad's house. "I'm going home."

He opened my door, grabbed me, pulled me out of the driver's seat, and pinned me to the back of the car. Then he searched the interior. At some point, his partner who had been sitting in the squad car joined him. The first officer asked me again where my identification was, and I told him it was in my gym bag, in the trunk—which he then opened.

That's when they pulled their guns on me.

"Get your identification out," one of them commanded.

With every passing second, a realization was sinking in: *I was in a situation.* In my head, I began hearing my dad telling me to stay calm and not make any sudden movements. As I was reaching for my bag, I told them I didn't have any weapons. I moved slowly. I emptied the contents of my bag out where they could see. My hands shook when I pulled my ID from my wallet. Because I was only seventeen my legal address was still at my mom's house, in a nearby neighborhood. Not the neighborhood I was in.

The officer challenged me, of course, and I stammered through an explanation. My parents were divorced. I was driving to my dad's house. All of it. One of the officers kept me pinned to the car while the other called in my ID. Eventually, they let me go—but not without writing me a criminal speeding ticket and citing me for failure to stop at both stop signs.

In other words, they lied.

And then they followed me to Dad's house.

My dad got home sometime later. When he walked in, I was still shaking and crying in my room. He demanded to know what was wrong. I told him everything, and I'll never forget his reaction. He looked me in the eyes, and he *smiled*.

"Welcome to being a Black man in America," he said.

I don't know what I was expecting—maybe for him to storm up to the police station and demand fair treatment for his son the way my mom had once stormed up to my elementary school—but I wasn't expecting him to be *amused* that it had finally happened to me.

For him, this was an opportunity for another lesson—in working hard and excellence even when life is truly unfair. Up to that point I had experienced racism, but never like that. I simply hadn't been exposed to that part of reality. Dad saw the experience as a wake-up call, something I could learn from. He believed that was something I needed, so I could learn to take injustice in stride and move on. Dad told me to sign up for the required driving classes. He made me pay all the fines, which I did by working at his office. He told me to figure out how to get out of the situation and get it done. It was time I realized that this was the world we live in.

If I was looking for relief from Mom, I wasn't going to get it there either. Mom and Dad were on the same page. Jerryd and I had grown up in largely White spaces, and both of them knew how important it was for the two of us to come to terms with the risks of being a young Black man in this country.

Some of us will experience more resistance from society than others. There are traps built into the road to success, and they don't look the same for everyone. That's the simple, unvarnished truth of being Black, or brown, or female, or impoverished in America. It's important to protect ourselves from this resistance, but it's also important not to let those experiences define our entire worldview—because that could shut us off from valuable potential connections.

For instance, my sophomore year, I walked into my new AP math class. The teacher took one look at me and told me I was in the wrong place. I wasn't, of course, and to her credit she apologized when I proved that to her. This moment of discrimination, though, led to a long history of allyship on her part. For many years after graduating, she was someone I reached out to when looking for opportunities to give back. She actually gave me my first opportunity to teach entrepreneurship to high school seniors, which planted the seed for many things to come in this book. So many of my experiences have come full circle like that.

I've also had a number of very positive experiences with the police in the years since I was pulled over. Once, many years after I began my journey to improve mental health in the community, a police officer actually apologized for pulling me over and thanked me for my work.

But those experiences were still years away. I still had to make it through high school, and that wasn't going to be easy—not with the dean of students having it out for me. My Catholic high school had strict rules about appearance and dress. Some of the discipline was good, but they weren't culturally appropriate. For instance, males were expected to come to school clean-shaven every day. That kind of rule can cause a lot of skin problems for a young Black man with different hair and dermatological needs, and such was my experience. The dean of students didn't care. He sought me out first thing every morning and hit me with a summons if I hadn't shaved that day. Each summons cost me twenty dollars. If I accrued enough of them, I'd have after-school detention. My parents had to get involved and convince the school to give me some leeway on the dress code. But the dean of students found other ways to punish me. He suspended me for a week once for getting into my dad's car in the wrong pickup lane after school. Those kinds of issues continued until I graduated.

Expectations and Early Entrepreneurship

Despite the pressures I was under, I continued to excel, and as I hit the back half of my high school career, attention was beginning to turn toward next steps. In career counseling with the nuns at my high school, I was being pushed to go into the military. Specifically, they seemed to think I'd be a good fit for the Air Force.

I was somewhat attracted to the idea at first—after all, a number of my family members on Dad's side were Air Force vets—but my parents were completely affronted by it. I remember asking Mom what would be so wrong with enlisting and eventually flying fighter jets.

Mom looked at my now six-and-a-half-foot-plus frame. "First of all," she said, "can you even fit in a cockpit?"

She had me there.

Looking back now, I understand my parents' indignation. It was ridiculous that I was being pushed toward military service when my ambitions clearly led in a very different direction. The truth is that many teachers and administrators throughout my school career never considered the levels I could reach. Steady and dependable work was at the forefront of their minds, not pushing for excellence.

With a military career off the table, I turned my attention to colleges, and I had one in particular in mind: Stanford. I never kept my dream of going to Stanford a secret—even though sharing it always earned me a laugh. A lot of people automatically assumed I wouldn't be able to go to a top institution.

Stanford or not, though, my aptitude and interest in business had been clear since childhood. Beyond the birthday gifts of stocks and the summer school classes on finance, I'd already proven I had a good head for math and a latent skill for sensing a good business opportunity.

Way back in seventh grade, I'd run an enterprise from my school locker, selling candy to my fellow students. This was the summer after I took my first personal finance class, and I must have been on the lookout for an opportunity to start making money. Shopping with Mom at Costco one day, I noticed how cheap candy was to buy in bulk. Why not buy cheap and sell high to all my hungry classmates?

My mom, amused by the hustle, had been happy to take me to Costco to pick up supplies after school so I could run the enterprise. But the same principal who suspended me for fighting back when kids were harassing me was far less amused. He thought I was selling drugs at first. Even though he was demonstrably wrong, he suspended me again anyway. Knowing my suspension was completely ridiculous, Mom brought home California Pizza Kitchen for me every day I was out of school. My math teacher, Mr. Stidham, was also on my side. He loved my candy hustle.

So despite my suspension, my first business effort was a positive experience. And from that point on, I was always looking for the next side hustle.

I found it after I met my buddy Vince in high school. Vince played football and was the only other minority kid in the AP classes with me. We were the two kids who didn't quite fit anywhere, so we fit together. And at some point, we went from friends to business partners.

Around the time our friendship was hitting its stride, a new tech platform called Napster started getting traction. For those of you too young to remember, Napster was a file-sharing program—one used mostly to share free music. Vince and I figured we could use it to launch our own business. We were able to get new albums before they dropped publicly, burn them onto compact disks, and sell them at school. We even sold them at my dad's office after school. It was the first time I was hustling *with* someone, and I loved the dynamic of working with others to realize an idea. While it was short-lived, it was yet another sign of where my talents and interests truly lay.

The Road to Morehouse

It turns out, I didn't get into Stanford. But as a great student and varsity captain of a great basketball team, I had a lot of colleges to choose from. My number one goal—like most kids at eighteen—was to get out of my home state and gain some independence. I was incredibly excited to leave. After the Stanford rejection, my main focus was to find a good school in SoCal where I could play basketball and have a good time for four years. There were plenty of suiters, but my heart was set on one of Loyola Marymount in LA, University of San Diego, or San Diego State University.

Unfortunately, my workouts for all three were terrible, and I likely cost myself a full scholarship. Schools in Arizona offered me everything—full ride and presidential scholarships—but that couldn't outweigh the fact that they were in Arizona. It looked like if I wanted to play ball and go to California, I'd have to come up with some cash to cover whatever the partial scholarships wouldn't.

As I considered my options, a new opportunity came forward: a small, historically Black private school in Atlanta called Morehouse College.

I'd only applied to Morehouse because of a visit with my dad's family in Atlanta when I was fifteen. We stayed with my dad's cousin, Ila, and her husband, Bob, and did a sightseeing tour of Atlanta history. We saw the Martin Luther King, Jr. National Historical Park and the Coca-Cola factory, and then we drove through the Atlanta University Center.

"Oh, that's Morehouse," Ila told me. "It would probably be great for you, Justin. You should apply there." Ila has this amazing spirit—she's really such a wonderful person—and her suggestion meant something to me. I thought I'd enjoy seeing more of my dad's family, too, who we didn't visit all that often.

Ila and Justin

After we got back, Dad began pushing Morehouse as an option, but I wasn't that interested. Morehouse was definitely a dark horse choice. After losing Stanford and only getting partial scholarship offers from my SoCal dream schools, though, I was willing to at least entertain Dad's preference.

Morehouse sweetened its offer by providing me something different from all the other out-of-state schools: a full *academic* presidential scholarship. There, I'd only have to pay for books and food. Attending Morehouse meant giving up basketball, but by that time, I was coming to the realization that I didn't love the game enough to make a career out of it.

Further motivating me was the movie *Drumline* that had just come out. It featured Nick Cannon as a kid who relocates from New York to a fictional, historically Black college in Atlanta. I'd recently seen the movie and thought the move to Atlanta sounded appealing.

So while I agreed to visit at least partly to get Dad off my back, I can't say I wasn't intrigued by the possibility.

But it was the trip itself that truly blew me away.

Ila and Bob picked Dad and I up from the airport. At that point in my life, Bob was the most brilliant person I'd ever met. He had a PhD in economics from Tufts, had started multiple businesses, and had been a consultant for a lot of big companies. Bob attended the family weekend events with Dad and me. We visited different departments and then attended Crown Forum, where we heard Oprah speak on business. We also got a peek at the "Pearly Gates," the nickname we had for the entrance to Spelman College, the historically all-Black female college next door.

These were all incredible experiences, but what really struck me was that Morehouse looked different than any place I'd ever been before. Everywhere I looked, young Black men were professionally dressed, moving through the campus fueled by the purpose behind their education. The sheer number of young Black men on a mission in a suit and tie, having a good time while focused on excelling, was astounding to me. I suddenly realized that joining the program at Morehouse would mean I was no longer the "dark horse" at school. All around me were kids from Chicago, LA, and New York who'd taken education seriously and were trying to perform. The environment felt so comfortable. I finally felt like I'd found a place to fit in.

We all went to dinner that night—Bob, Ila, their daughter Gabrielle and son Brandon, Dad, and me. I looked around the table and thought, *These people are gonna take care of me.* Then Bob started discussing Morehouse, waxing poetic on its opportunities and famous graduates, really sealing the deal.

I have my suspicions that Dad orchestrated this whole event, all the way down to the speeches at dinner. What he didn't know, though, was that it was all unnecessary. I'd already decided I was going to Morehouse.

Getting Down to Business

Mom was initially concerned about my Morehouse decision. It was very sudden and came right after my visit. So she had reason to worry I was being impulsive. At the same time, it was my father's choice, and it was so far from home. But she came around after speaking to her godfather, whose son had gone to Morehouse and who recommended the institution highly. Still, when I left, I think she felt she was losing me to Dad.

She wasn't entirely wrong. The Morehouse visit did change my relationship with Dad. The words he told me on that trip would guide much of my young life from that point forward.

"It's not about making your family proud anymore," he told me. "It's about making yourself proud. So go out and make yourself proud."

At Morehouse, I was more determined than ever to succeed. I was the guy in the dorm studying, keeping my head down like Dad taught me. I took it so seriously. I'd heard too many horror stories about other people who'd failed, and I would do almost anything to avoid that fate.

My efforts paid off. I excelled in Morehouse's hardest business classes and garnered attention and recommendations from the toughest professors—in particular, Professor Emmanuel Onifade, who would play a key role in jump-starting my career. I never had the quintessential "college experience," but by working hard and putting my dad's lessons into practice, I put my goals within reach. Even then, I knew that sacrifice was huge. Every entrepreneur has to sacrifice to get where they want to be. There's no such thing as a work/life balance. It's a work/life *priority*.

I wasn't the only one at Morehouse who understood that. Kyle Polk understood it as well—although he definitely put a bit more emphasis on the living part than I did at the time. I met Kyle my freshman year. He lived on the floor above me in the dorms. He was in the business department like me, had a connection to Detroit, and lived in my building. We took a lot of the same classes and had some shared interests, but we didn't immediately hit it off.

Kyle's been my best friend my entire adult life—a source of support and advice whom I still speak to multiple times every week—but we're very different types of people. I'm naturally quite reserved, while Kyle is always the life of the party. I can be a bit more pessimistic, while Kyle is usually very optimistic. Considering that we're somewhat opposites of each other, it makes sense that it took a little time for our friendship to really develop. Second semester, though, I got the chance to move off campus to this incredible loft in downtown Atlanta. Kyle became a regular guest. We started hosting people at my place and chasing girls at Spelman together. We worked hard, but our friendship really blossomed in finding ways to have fun.

There was more to our friendship—the reasons we clicked—than that, of course. Kyle had been raised by his grandfather, the Reverend Armistice Roosevelt Polk, a very prominent figure in the African Methodist Episcopal Church who had been an important leader in the Civil Rights Movement throughout the sixties and seventies. Kyle had grown up inspired by his grandfather and desiring to make an impact on his community—a motivation I shared. My father had made a huge difference to the Black community in Phoenix, and already I knew that no matter his words, I wanted to do more than be a success for my own sake. Kyle and I may have enjoyed the party scene, but we were both fired by the need to become servant leaders that elevated our community.

Justin and Morehouse Classmates at Martin Luther King's
Historic Home in Atlanta, GA House (Kyle Polk center)

Parties, girls, hip-hop, and a shared motivation would be enough to create a lifelong friendship, but the bond between Kyle and I went even deeper than that. Though neither of us knew it, Kyle and I had *history*. The summer after our freshman year, Kyle came to visit me in Phoenix where I was working an internship. Not only had we become close, but Kyle had also formed a relationship with my dad, who came out to Atlanta often. Kyle's father wasn't in the picture, and "Papa Bayless" would come to fill that role in many ways for him. He and my dad shared a similar energy: big, charismatic, and magnetic. That's probably another reason Kyle and I worked. In coming out to see me, then, Kyle could hang out with me and with "Papa Bayless," as he called my father.

Kyle arrived for the week of Fourth of July in Phoenix, and we decided to attend my grandfather's barbecue. It promised to be a lot of fun, but not particularly because of the host. Grandad wasn't someone who screamed "fun." He was still the strong, quiet, disciplined first lieutenant who had gone to Germany four decades earlier. Needless to say, he was as no nonsense as it gets. If my dad and Kyle had similar spirits, Grandad was the opposite—which made what followed all the more extraordinary.

I was showing Kyle around "Fred's place"—an entire garage full of sports memorabilia, with old pictures from his life hanging on the walls. Kyle immediately started poring over the framed photos. Then, suddenly, he stopped and plucked one right off the wall.

"Bro, he's going to kill you," I gasped.

Kyle ignored me. Picture in hand, he pushed past me, walked straight up to my grandfather, and said, "Why is my grandfather on your wall?"

As it turned out, my grandfather's brother knew Kyle's grandfather. More than that, they were close friends and fellow pastors. My great uncle worked hand-in-hand with Reverend Armistice Roosevelt Polk in the African Methodist Episcopal Church in Detroit. Together, they'd helped organize volunteers who went south during the Civil Rights Movements. Together, they'd helped elect Coleman A. Young, the first Black mayor of Detroit.

No wonder Kyle and I got along so well. We'd clearly inherited a kindred spirit from our elders.

3

NEW YORK STATE OF MIND

In many ways, my story of success has always been a story about mentorship. That's why this book begins with my father and my mother—my first and greatest mentors. But they aren't the only ones. Throughout my early education there were always teachers who saw my ability and nurtured my potential.

But until I entered Morehouse in the fall of 2003, I had never been in an environment where I could really be my full self—and the mentors I met could push me toward the path I was best suited for.

For the first time in my life, I felt entirely comfortable in my environment. With basketball in my rearview and nothing else to divert my focus, I flourished. I felt completely and unreservedly supported in my academic pursuits, and I began learning with a ferocity that I never had before.

Perhaps that's why I felt comfortable enrolling in Professor Onifade's accounting class my first year. The class was for sophomores—and was considered challenging even then—but I had earned enough AP credits in high school to qualify. Professor Onifade is a wise but extremely intense and intimidating instructor. A survivor of a war zone, he has scars on his face from his early life in Nigeria. After coming to America, he would earn all his degrees and eventually become director of the accounting program. He brought a seriousness of purpose to his courses. He told our class that if we messed around, we'd fail. And he seemed to be as good as his word. The rumor was that half of the people who took his course failed it.

But there I was, far and away the youngest in the class, finding the material *easy*.

Of course, I had always had a good head for math. That's one of the reasons Mom had enrolled me in a summer program for personal finance in the first place. And I'd already shown promise in business calculus, but Professor Onifade's class was where I really came to shine.

I think the key was less my innate mathematical skills than the fact I wasn't intimidated by the professor. Most students try to avoid the hard teachers, but I saw the professor as a potential mentor. This was an opportunity.

Embracing the challenge, I was able to gather so much wisdom. Professor Onifade taught me the true value of the African proverb, "A bird in the hand is worth two in the bush." While there would be times ahead when I had to ignore that wisdom, it's continued to make me mindful of the risk of throwing away what I have for what I might want. But his greatest gift was recognizing my potential and advising me on the direction I should take my academic and future career.

"You have a talent here," he said to me one day. "You should become an accountant."

This wasn't what I wanted to hear. "I don't really want to do taxes for a living," I protested.

"Accounting is the language of business," he countered. "I want to set up some meetings with other professors and the college to talk about your plan."

Professor Onifade was right. Accounting skills would prove valuable over time. In fact, training as an accountant would help me deal with one of the great difficulties of entrepreneurship:

tackling cash flow and understanding the underlying unit economics of the business. Professor Onifade helped me learn the principles behind parsing financial statements and managing a general ledger far earlier than most people in business.

It was great advice—but I didn't take it right away. Instead, I was noncommittal. A few days later, I talked to Bob, and it was only when he backed up the professor's point that I was willing to admit they were both probably right. After that conversation, I switched from my major of chemical engineering to accounting.

Backing up his belief in me, Professor Onifade also put me on the track to success in the corporate world. Because of the excellence and drive I'd shown in his class, he made a point of introducing me to the people who could make my career. After finishing my freshman year with a 4.0 grade average, Professor Onifade also introduced me to Benjamin P. McLaurin, director of Morehouse's Career Services division.

He was the man with all the relationships to all the companies looking for talent at Morehouse. When I interviewed with him, he had only one warning for me: "Don't embarrass us. Remember, you represent this college first and foremost."

Once I told him I had no intention of in any way embarrassing the college, he began putting me in touch with several Fortune 500 companies. Whenever business industry powerhouses—banks, consulting groups, or advisory firms such as PricewaterhouseCoopers—came to Morehouse looking for the best and brightest, my name was at the top of the list.

This is the power of committing to your work with dedication. If you give everything, others will notice, and many will be inspired to invest in you. Doors will start to open.

A year later, I experienced the benefits of this support. Although the major New York banks don't typically hire summer interns before their junior year, I applied my sophomore year—thanks to the encouragement of Professor Onifade and Mr. McLaurin.

Things happened rather quickly after that. In February, Credit Suisse First Boston sent a recruiter to campus to meet me. We sat down together, and she talked to me about Wall Street. A week later, they flew me to New York City, all expenses paid.

I had never been to NYC before, and navigating the city bustle to arrive at my room at the Marriott Marquis in Times Square was incredibly inspiring. In the midst of churning sidewalks and traffic noise, I felt overcome at the prospect ahead. I was staring at an opportunity no one in my family had ever had: an interview day with a major player in world finance in the center of the Big Apple.

Not that this was some fairy-tale event. An interview day is exactly what it sounds like: a grueling, eight-hour day of interviews with as many personnel in as many departments as possible. They quizzed me on my knowledge and interviewed me to see if I had the personality to handle the work. The process is designed to see if a potential candidate will be able to "make it on the Street," and if they can, where they belong in the organization. If I was successful, I'd leave New York with a summer internship at Credit Suisse First Boston and an additional scholarship—an accomplishment that's harder to achieve than getting into Harvard or Stanford.

I arrived at Twenty-Third Street and Madison Avenue and ran Credit Suisse's gauntlet of interviews. At the end of the day, exhausted and elated, I left with the intuition that my first trip to New York wouldn't be my last. The very next day, Credit Suisse First Boston called to offer me my first internship on Wall Street. That same year, I joined Phi Beta Kappa as the first Morehouse student to ever be received as a sophomore. Thus began my journey of scholastic recognition at Morehouse, which culminated in winning basically every business scholarship and academic honor they had on offer.

At the end of my sophomore year, I returned to New York, hungry to learn and flourish on Wall Street. Over the twelve weeks of my internship, I met several individuals who would help mentor me through this incredibly important part of my professional development. Gardy Berthomieux, my first boss, was the first to really believe in me on the Street. He introduced me to other leaders at Credit Suisse First Boston, including Verdun Perry, a Black executive director at the time who would later become the global head of Blackstone Strategic Partners, one of the largest secondary financial funds in the world.

My mom suggested I also reach out to someone she'd gone to high school with: Derek Jones, an executive director in private equity at the time, who is now the vice chairman for Grosvenor GCM, an investment firm focused on diverse capital fund managers. All three men provided me with crucial guidance that summer. They were an inspiration, being the first three Black men that I have ever seen accomplish a level of financial success akin to a celebrity or athlete. But their ultimate, lasting contribution to my rise came in the form of a recommendation.

One day, over lunch, when we were discussing next steps after my internship finished, Verdun made a suggestion. It caught my attention because it echoed what I'd already heard from Gardy and Derek.

"As a Black banker on Wall Street, if you want to reach the next level, there's a woman you should meet," he said. "She's tough. She can make or break a career. But I think you can handle it.

"Her name is Carla Harris."

The Godmother of Wall Street

Carla Harris is a woman whose reputation should really precede her. She is truly larger than life. The "godmother of Wall Street," she is likely the most successful Black woman to ever work in finance in America. She's been critical to the rise of many Black professionals, and she has been my mentor for decades. She can also be quite intimidating. She's powerful, and her energy is big and bold. She commands every room she enters. And she does not suffer fools. She is kind and nurturing and demanding in a way that a strict auntie would be. You know she loves you, but she won't hesitate to put you in your place.

That energy helped draw me across the room for our first introduction. I was at a meet and greet for Morgan Stanley—the kind of networking event New York banks hold to search out new talent—and Carla walked into the room.

I'd heard all the fears from my colleagues, but it never made sense to me to be afraid of her. As with Professor Onifade, I wasn't intimidated. If she had the power to ruin a career, she also had the power to *make* one. To me, that was a risk worth taking.

I didn't hesitate to introduce myself. I told her I went to Morehouse, and to my surprise, she already knew who I was. In fact, as someone who helped get Morgan Stanley's diversity initiatives off the ground and one of the architects of the Richard B. Fisher Scholarship program for students from underrepresented communities, she'd heard quite a bit about me.

"I'd love to sit down with you when I come to campus," she said. I readily agreed.

I knew that Carla could give me my big break. My mentors had collectively recommended a single best track to success: try to get a position in the top suite of banks. Their advice echoed that old song about New York. If I could make it at Morgan Stanley, I could make it anywhere.

If I could impress Carla when she came down to Morehouse, I'd truly be on my way.

Back at Morehouse I found that I had leapt ahead of my peers. While Kyle and all my other friends were looking to get their first real experience of the business world, I already had a Wall Street internship under my belt. I was already Phi Beta Kappa with a 4.0. When the big banks came recruiting, I was at the top of their list.

More importantly, I was at the top of Carla's list. She came to meet me early in the fall semester. We had a great meeting and suddenly my schedule was peppered with additional Morgan Stanley interviews. Within days, I had an offer from them for the following summer, which I accepted immediately. It wasn't clear which department I'd be working in, but I was given the chance to request my areas of interest. Carla's department—Equity Capital Markets—was my first choice.

Carla had made her name in capital markets. She had been involved in the pricing of UPS, one of the largest IPOs in US history. She had also taken Martha Stewart Living Omnimedia public, as well as Immunex, one of the largest biotech common stock transactions ever done in the market. In other words, she had very much earned her a reputation as "the deal maker."

Unfortunately, I wasn't placed under Carla. Instead, I was assigned to mortgage-backed securities. In 2006, the Street was doing an all-out blitz on mortgage-backed securities. It was one of the top profit centers at Morgan Stanley and would be for another year—until the housing bubble burst. Not knowing what lay ahead for the economy, I focused on the opportunity in front of me. I wasn't really interested in this area, but I still had a shot that many would die for. *I'm at Morgan Stanley*, I told myself. *Make it count.*

But I was soon to discover it wasn't all open doors and mentors on Wall Street. The office may have looked very different from the halls of the Phoenix grade schools that I attended, but some of the same attitudes lingered. A week into the internship, a VP gave me an assignment and told me not to "put any ghetto language into the presentation." I was shocked almost to silence.

"What does that mean?" I asked, looking him squarely in the face.

"You know what that means," he fired back.

Uncertain what else to do, I requested a meeting with Carla.

This time, I actually was terrified of going to see her. I didn't feel any better after I'd explained the situation. Her expression gave away *nothing*. She just stared me down.

"I'll be a hundred percent real with you," she said, her voice level. "I will look into what you just said. But first and foremost, are you working hard?"

Her question confused me. I'd never *not* worked hard a day in my life. My parents had brought me up better than that. *Of course* I was working hard.

"Are you putting in the effort?" she clarified. "If I were to ask the team if you're engaged, what are they going to say? Will they tell me you're screwing around?"

"No."

There was a pause. I could've fainted.

"Okay, then here's the deal. When I look into this, one of two things will happen. One, I'm going to find out you're telling the truth about showing up and doing everything you're supposed to. If that's the case, you'll start with me on Monday. Two," she continued, "if I find out you're lying and screwing around, you won't receive a full-time offer."

I left her office shaking, feeling like my entire career might be on the line. It was Friday afternoon. It was going to be a long weekend before I discovered my fate.

In the hopes of a positive outcome, I was at my desk early on Monday morning, already working before 6:30 when Carla usually arrived. She always expected her team to be the first in, ready to go and working before anyone else even got there. If I was going to be on her team, I had to show I knew the rules.

It paid off. That day she walked in, came straight to my desk, and told me to grab my stuff because I was going with her.

I was getting a seat on her lean, elite team—a seat that was more difficult to earn than acceptance to any Ivy League school. Right away she introduced me to the only other team members in Equity Capital Markets. And then there was me, a twenty-one-year-old summer intern, set up to learn from the best. I didn't know it then, but her analyst planned to leave the next year. I was being groomed to replace him.

Joining the Entrepreneurial Party

That summer at Morgan Stanley was one of the best times in my life. In addition to working on Carla's team, Kyle and my other Morehouse and Spelman friends were now in the city. We all worked hard, made good money, and had the time of our lives. I opted for student housing at Columbia, but Kyle had elected to rent a penthouse loft overlooking the Hudson River. After Kyle had spent half of freshman and sophomore year at my place in Atlanta, I figured I'd earned the right to spend my free time at his pad.

That wasn't all I spent.

Kyle and I were training under some of the best financial minds in America, but the irony was that instead of investing in the publicly traded companies we were learning how to finance—a move that could've built real wealth from the significant scholarship and stipend money we'd received—we were spending everything we had on expensive suits and lunch in swanky restaurants, trying to emulate the big Wall Street players we saw. We were young guys with money, picking up ATM receipts that were intentionally left for us to find by the seasoned bankers. It was common to see large balances of up to eight figures sitting in someone's account. Everywhere we looked, motivation to spend like a high roller was staring back.

I'd be lying if I said I didn't enjoy wearing nice suits and going to nice restaurants, but playing the game also had a secondary purpose. Kyle and I intended to shake things up, and to do that, we had to reach the top. We became something of a team, encouraging one another to succeed and to have fun while doing it.

Nothing showed the power of our relationship like the parties we threw. That summer marked a period of growth for Red Carpet Enterprises, an elite party-planning service we'd started the year before at Morehouse. Atlanta was the burgeoning new center of hip-hop, and we'd seen how recent Morehouse graduates had turned partying into business before. We decided it was our turn to get a cut. Essentially, Kyle and I would organize parties in quality locations, make sure the bar was stocked, and invite the right set of people. We'd get a cut from the door for our efforts. It proved to be quite a profitable business model, and a whole lot of fun. Our first party was at Club Cherry, and it was such a success, the fire marshal had to shut us down. What followed was a successful string of lavish parties on campus and in the Atlanta area.

New York represented a whole new ball game for us. We began with house parties in Kyle's penthouse, but by his twenty-first birthday on June 30 we were ready for something bigger. We rented a huge space in the Bowery district and threw an epic, Wall-Street-meets-fashion party that really put Red Carpet on the map. It was so epic, in fact, that it garnered the attention of the press.

And *that* got Carla's attention.

She came to my desk one morning after the Bowery party and threw the newspaper with our party's write-up down at me.

"Do you want to be known for doing deals or for throwing parties?" she seethed. "There's nothing wrong with parties, but if you want to be taken seriously on the Street, you can't afford for *this* to be what your reputation is built upon."

She was right, of course. It can be hard to change false impressions—especially when you're new. It was hard enough to make it in my position; getting a reputation as a partier could only make it harder.

Behind Carla's concern was a second, equally important question: Would I allow fun to sideline my career? It's a danger many young entrepreneurs encounter, and I can't say I entirely escaped it myself. Fun is a great temptation and a great motivator in entrepreneurship, but it can also be a distraction that pulls you away from the real work at hand.

It would be years before I completely cut the cord on my fun side project, but Carla convinced me to redouble my efforts at Morgan Stanley, keeping my head down the way Dad had always taught me. His speech about making myself proud had stayed with me, and I wanted to prove to him that I could do that.

Apparently, I did enough to prove myself to Carla as well. At the end of my internship, she invited me to lunch. She asked where I wanted to go and what I wanted to do. I didn't hesitate.

"I only want to work at Morgan Stanley," I said. "But I also only want to work with you. If there isn't room in your department, I'll look elsewhere."

"You really have a big brass set of balls," she chuckled, "but I think I can make that happen."

By Labor Day I had an offer to join her team full time immediately after graduation.

The Bubble Bursts

I finished all the courses for my degree early at Morehouse. Unfortunately, there was no time to kick back. As soon as Carla discovered I'd finished early, she told me to get back to New York. That meant that unlike my friends who were enjoying their final semester, I was working eighty- and ninety-hour weeks for Carla. She was relentless in her work ethic, and that meant I had to be too. I was young enough—and there was caffeine enough—to just about keep up.

On Halloween of 2007, though, everything began to fall apart. It wasn't on my end; it was the world that was breaking. I was sitting at my desk around midnight preparing the Burger King follow-on IPO for the market opening the next day. Someone dropped a copy of *Bloomberg* magazine in front of me. On the cover, I saw sprawling headlines about "toxic debt" and the mortgage crisis.

By then, I'd become Carla's analyst. I was now part of a group of five, with Carla as managing director. We were far enough removed from my old department, mortgage-backed securities, that we hadn't yet heard many rumblings about a looming financial crisis. But then Morgan Stanley suddenly began letting people go. In the blink of an eye, Carla's vice president was gone.

That left Carla, and me, to run the entire desk.

I remember calling my mom when it happened. I was so scared that I was almost in tears. The hours I was working were already taking a toll on my body. I didn't see how I would be able to absorb the work of another person all by myself and survive. I knew Carla wouldn't slow down. Her energy and work ethic were set to a constant go, go, go.

Honestly, I wasn't sure I wanted to push any harder at Morgan Stanley. Two weeks after the vice president was let go, I walked in to see a big blue sign had been placed on the wall: "How much money did you make today?"

Perhaps it was just some individual banker trying to motivate themselves through the crisis. We were positioned on the capital markets floor, after all, and such cutthroat personal mantras were not uncommon. Still, it gnawed at me.

Is that all that matters? I wondered. I had entered this profession because I wanted to make money—but I also wanted to make money *do something* for people. I wanted money to accomplish something for our families and our communities. That wasn't what the world of Wall Street looked like through my eyes in 2007. People were starting to lose their jobs, their savings, and their homes. Yet all some people around me cared about was making money. I wanted to do something more than that. And I was beginning to suspect I'd have to look elsewhere if I wanted to make my career matter.

A Vision in Phoenix

In November of 2007 I started traveling between New York and Arizona to watch my brother Jerryd play basketball for the University of Arizona in Tucson. I developed a strategy to take a Friday evening flight out to Phoenix, get a ride down to Tucson and back, and then take the Sunday night red-eye back to New York. On my first trip out, I was shocked to see both my parents waiting at the airport to pick me up. Things had been bitter between them ever since their divorce. While they'd become more civil with one another in recent years, I wasn't expecting to see them standing together, waiting to drive me down to see Jerryd—in the same car.

That first trip to Tucson, the three of us stayed in the same hotel. We shared our first meal together in a long, long time. Jerryd's potential professional career was becoming more and more certain, and their shared desire to protect him had fostered real change in their relationship. The bitterness was gone. For the first time since my childhood, it felt like they were friends. And it felt like they were on the same team.

They weren't just on Team Jerryd either. Dad had plans for me, and Mom was happy to let him have the floor.

Little did I know at the time, but Dad had his heart set on convincing me to join his company and eventually take over. He'd mentioned to his old friend and colleague, the psychologist Dr. Jon McCaine, that he'd come to believe my business skills could be transformative for the company.

On a separate car ride around that time, he had said to Jon, "Listen, am I crazy or is this kid seeing things that I'm not seeing? He just seems to understand the business on a level I don't."

Jon had agreed, "I don't think you're crazy. I think he's your guy."

I certainly couldn't have been better prepared to take on a role. Though I don't think Dad planned it this way, he'd basically brought me up at his office. Dad was always working, and I naturally began taking on responsibilities myself from an early age just to spend a little time with him. From age nine, I was in the office (wearing a suit I'd demanded so I could look like Dad), shredding documents and organizing files.

During the summer, I went to lunch with him every day at his favorite restaurant, Alexi's Grill.

From then on, every year, he had me do something different. Front desk, enrollment—I made my way through every aspect of administration in the office. I knew the functions. I knew all the problems. I spoke the language, and I knew the team. Unbeknownst to either of us, I'd spent my youth onboarding to take over one day.

By late 2007, it was no longer unbeknownst to Dad. He was well aware, and he began a campaign to recruit me. Every car ride from Tucson to Phoenix over the next several months included a speech about mental health and the possibilities he saw for Bayless & Associates if I left Wall Street. "You call yourself a businessman," he'd say. "What kind of businessman are you if you can't look at the family business, with your name on the sign, and see the value we can realize for the world?"

I might not have taken him seriously at first, but I was listening. Dad was excellent at casting a vision. Just as his words had convinced Goldwater to back him and influenced my Morehouse decision, they struck a chord now. If I was getting tired of the endless hours solely focused on profit, was this the solution?

In February 2008, I asked Carla for some time off. I'd been running hard—we all had—and she gave me the week to catch my breath. I flew back to Phoenix where the city was hosting the Super Bowl. In one of the most unbelievable moments of my life, we actually got to go to the game. It happened like this. On the Saturday before kickoff, I was hanging out with my cousin Merv, hungover from our Friday night out. His mom, my aunt Stephanie, came in with my dad, and I somewhat flippantly suggested, "Hey, we should go to the game tomorrow."

My dad was having none of it. "Are you kidding? I am not paying for that."

Cousin Stephanie, though, was now also Congresswoman Stephanie. She picked up the phone, dialed some number, and asked for four tickets to the game. Ten minutes later, she got a call back. Because of her, I was sitting three rows up on the fifty-yard line when David Tyree made the famous "Helmet Catch" that gave the New York Giants the win over the New England Patriots.

It was obviously a great moment for an Arizona boy working in the Big Apple—and a lesson in what real power looks like from Cousin Stephanie. But the week was important for another reason. It was then that I began having serious conversations with my dad about joining Bayless & Associates.

Dad had believed providing at-home mental healthcare would be a game changer since the 1980s, but he lacked the necessary skill set to make that dream a reality. I had the business acumen and thought that I understood how to scale a business, but I didn't fully understand the medical and health insurance side of the business. In other words, we needed each other.

By then, I had assessed Bayless & Associates from every business angle. I knew people needed services, and I thought I had a strategy that could bring the company closer to Dad's goal. This was early 2008, when everyone seemed focused on the aging baby boomer population. I took the idea to my dad.

"Why don't you offer any services to geriatric populations? It seems like there's major potential in working with them."

He just looked at me from behind his desk, a knowing smile on his face. Then he opened a drawer, pulled out a file, and tossed it to me. It was full of contracts from UnitedHealthcare, Aetna, Centene, and other major health-care providers. All the contracts were for geriatric adults with chronic mental health illnesses for whom the state had agreed to provide long-term care services.

"People have been asking me to put behavioral services together for these older adults in skilled nursing facilities for a while," he said.

"Why haven't you done it?"

"Because then *I'm* the energy," he said. "And that's what *you* should be."

That was how I found myself standing in a skilled nursing facility, wearing my Wall Street pinstripe suit, waiting for a meeting with an administrator who could help me untangle the ins and outs of behavioral health services for seniors.

The meeting was an eye-opening experience. What I saw when I entered the building was the stuff of chaos and tragedy. To this day it remains one of the saddest things I've ever seen. The administrator arrived late to our meeting, sweating profusely. The state was about to close their doors, their primary care and medical providers were about to leave, they had no psychiatric help, and their three hundred residents were truly suffering.

Right away I started asking questions about their facilities, their corporate ownership, and other facilities like this one. I left that meeting with the knowledge that fifty thousand geriatric residents of skilled nursing facilities—an entire population—were going without the mental health services they so desperately needed. No one was doing that at scale.

I knew I could put together a value proposition for the insurance companies that would lower the cost of care and improve the quality of outcomes for the senior population. These were publicly traded companies, after all. I already spoke their language. The wheels in my brain spun relentlessly onward as I considered the possibilities of telemedicine, administrative infrastructure, and how to change the course of Bayless & Associates.

I went back to Dad and told him to make me an offer. He wrote $60,000 on a piece of paper and slid it across his desk to me.

"Dad. That's less than 50 percent of what I'll make in New York."

"I don't care," he said. "This is what I'll pay you. And by the time you turn thirty, the company will be yours."

Back to Basketball?

That wasn't my only offer on the table.

While everything at Bayless & Associates was unfolding, Jerryd was preparing to go pro. As a result, Red Carpet morphed into a company that threw marketing parties for him and the NBA. My network of contacts in professional sports widened, and I began to feel pressure to piggyback on Jerryd's career and work on the business side of sports.

When I moved to New York I'd become friends with Kris Stone of *SLAM* magazine. Kris was best friends with NBA All-Star Jason Kidd, who had long been a family friend. Kris took me under his wing, bringing me to *Sports Illustrated* parties and showing me around the city. He was also aware of Jerryd's talent and had arranged for him to be featured in a 2008 documentary, *Gunnin' for That #1 Spot*, which he produced alongside Adam Yauch of the Beastie Boys. Kris would go on to be head of basketball marketing at Under Armour and eventually help to sign Steph Curry to represent the brand.

I know Kris meant well—we remain very close friends—but at the time, it felt to me like Kris was assuming my career would take a back seat to Jerryd's and that I'd find a way to work in the same area. I was also in contact with Jeff Schwartz, owner of Excel Sports—now the largest sports agency in the US. Jeff also represented Jason Kidd, and he encouraged me to leave Wall Street for a career in sports entertainment. Jeff thought it could be a great opportunity for me to help Jerryd with his career.

Kris and I started going to Chelsea Piers to play basketball and discuss opportunities in sports. Eventually Jeff made me an offer to come over to his firm as a junior agent, but as with Dad's offer, the salary was less than what I was making at Morgan Stanley. And truth be told, my heart wasn't really in it.

Crossroads

As I considered the road ahead, I had three options.

I could continue my prestigious career with Morgan Stanley, where I would make significant money despite feeling deep down that I should be doing something more than just making other people money. I could embark upon an open-ended career in sports entertainment full of opportunities I had yet to uncover, knowing this was the most common path for the siblings of successful athletes. Or I could leave prestige behind to try to scale my father's small mental health business.

I was torn between mentors. My father was pushing one way, and Carla pushed the other. Dad's case was strong, but so was Carla's. She suggested that I ought to stick around for a few more years to really learn the ropes. I could stay on the Street for a while, then maybe get an MBA at Harvard. I'd still be young by the time I went back to Arizona. I could make an impact in New York City *and* still have decades to make one in Phoenix.

It was a powerful argument. So what made me choose my father's company? It was undeniably the biggest risk and the least likely to prove lucrative. And as Carla had said, there was plenty of time to go back later. The downsides were so obvious, it was hard to believe I was even considering it. Yet, here was my chance to truly be an entrepreneur and make an impact.

There was huge growth potential in the industry and a chance to make a difference for my community. And I wouldn't have to spend my life staring at a sign asking how much money I'd made that day.

Or maybe it was just that my dad was that good a salesman. Whatever the reason, I chose Bayless & Associates.

I've never been more terrified in my professional life than when I went to Carla's office in March of 2008 and told her I planned to resign in two months' time to run my family business. Incredibly, she gave me her blessing.

"You've got to do what your heart tells you," she said.

As it turned out, Carla herself was contemplating starting a new venture inside of Morgan Stanley that would serve small asset managers of color. She would later go on to become the first Black vice chairwoman on Wall Street and the first African American to serve on Morgan Stanley's Management Committee. In the years since, she's continued to be one of my most valuable and cherished mentors—a person like Kyle whom I can reach out to regularly in order to get an honest response to my ambitions and ideas. Anything that involves investment, Wall Street, or strategy, I get her thoughts on before I make my final decision.

That was all ahead though. At the time, my focus turned to my resignation letter, and then to the email manifesto I previewed in the Introduction, full of references to Black Wall Street and ideas about changing the world. It was ambitious beyond any reason. I was calling my shot—and I was shooting behind the half-court line. I circulated that email to everyone I had a relationship with. I asked for investments, but no one believed in my project.

Almost everyone simply laughed and forgot about it. All my friends from Morehouse and Spelman who'd also made it on Wall Street—including Kyle—found my intentions more amusing than serious.

They weren't the last ones to laugh either. But each time someone laughed, that added to the chip I'd already developed on my shoulder. It was the same chip I'd had since childhood when my potential had been dismissed and limited by people. That chip had grown every time someone had waved away my ambitions. This was just more motivation to show everyone how wrong they were.

4

THE OTHER BROTHER

My last day at Morgan Stanley was May 30, 2008. Before I left New York, I took two weeks off to enjoy the city I'd only ever really seen at night. I decided to play the part of a tourist in the place I'd been living for the better part of two years. The biggest sight was seeing Jerryd drafted to the NBA in mid-June. Even at the draft, though, people giggled at my decision to walk away from prestige and take the less-obvious path.

I tried to ignore it, but all the time that chip on my shoulder was growing ever larger.

The day after the draft I flew back to Phoenix, where Red Carpet hosted a post-draft party for Jerryd. Within days, I'd signed the title for my first house. And then on July 1, 2008—just a week after the draft—I began work at Bayless & Associates.

Dad introduced me at the Monday morning staff meeting he had at the beginning of every month. He was a creature of habit, and he liked everything to follow the schedule he'd set for himself years before. He went to Alexi's Grill or one other favorite spot for all his lunch meetings, and he always had a Monday morning all-hands meeting.

"How long is the meeting?" I asked.

He shrugged. "As long as I want it to be."

Working on Wall Street taught me that staff meetings were formal events, so on the day of the meeting I dressed in a three-piece pinstripe suit. Walking in, I saw the first sign I'd need to reexamine my assumptions. Everyone else was dressed casually—some even in Birkenstocks. Far from looking professional, I looked like I didn't belong.

I had a long time to dwell on that fact. I soon learned *as long as I want it to be* translated to three hours of Dad talking. Not that anyone complained. Everyone there loved Dad. Along with his magnetic personality, he was also incredibly loyal to his people—even to a fault. If someone messed up and went against the standards of mental healthcare, he could be vicious, but otherwise, he didn't enforce much accountability. In fact, he'd given almost all authority for the company to the social worker heading the children's clinic. This was great for employee morale, but it meant there was almost no efficiency to be found. On Friday afternoons, everyone abandoned work altogether to hang out in Dad's office and chitchat amid a haze of cigar and cigarette smoke and lava lamps.

At the center of it all—from the Monday morning meetings to the Friday afternoon chitchat—was Dad. Everyone was drawn to him. He was so charismatic, so charming, he held everyone's attention as long as he wanted it. In some respects, it was great to see, but in others, it represented an obstacle. Because if all the light was shining on him, there wasn't much left over for me.

In Two Shadows

It wasn't just the culture that was shocking; it was also my position. In New York, I'd been a rising star that people paid attention to. I worked for one of the top people on Wall Street. I wasn't necessarily important, but I was on my way.

Back in Phoenix, I was clearly in Dad's shadow. He had this aura about him. He was so engaging that he owned every room he entered. And he was such an expert, particularly in forensics, that doctoral graduates from all over the country came to learn from him before going out to open their own practices. I walked into that office with a wealth of experience, an excellent education, and a ten-year plan to take over the business, but none of that seemed to matter. When Dad was in the room, no one was going to listen to me. The staff at Bayless & Associates returned Dad's loyalty tenfold. No one was looking to me for leadership.

Even as I began to build administrative infrastructure behind the company, the clinicians and staff continued to turn to him for everything. And why wouldn't they? The company still had his full name in the title: Michael B. Bayless & Associates.

I also didn't help myself initially. I am actually a natural ambivert. As a trained accountant and financial analyst, I was sometimes more comfortable with data than business social gatherings. I could relax and have fun, but I was most at home running numbers and building models for success. Those skills had allowed me to shine at Morehouse and on the Street. But they wouldn't cut it anymore.

A few months into my new career, the company was having a Christmas party. While everyone else was making merry, I was in my office, building a model for how to reorganize some aspect of the company. Suddenly, Dad burst in.

"What are you doing? You think you're going to be a leader hiding behind this computer? You need to stop being a financial robot, get out there, and find out what makes these people tick."

I did as I was told, but at that time, I still didn't fully grasp how important my dad's message was. I despised his Monday morning and Friday afternoon meetings. All I saw was how much time they wasted. It would be years before I saw the real value lurking behind all that inefficiency.

I did begin to change though. From then on, I put more effort into participating in things. I followed my dad's lead and made the effort to spend time every day walking the office, speaking to people. But it was a long road ahead to truly secure buy-in.

That made it difficult to take on a number of major shifts the company had to make if it was to be more successful. Dad had run the business for decades with independent contractors who needed to be transitioned into W-2 employees. That was just one of many changes necessary if we wanted to get the company out of "no-man's land"—when a company is trapped between $1 million and $10 million in revenue. The path to a $1 million company is fairly straightforward. Likewise, if you can get to $10 million, scaling usually gets easier. The most difficult stretch is the "no-man's land" in between. I had my work cut out for me to bridge that distance—especially when I was constantly overshadowed by Dad. At this time, the company was approximately $1.5 million in annual revenue.

Dad's shadow followed me out of the office as well. Growing up in Phoenix, I was coming back to a group of friends. But I was so young, many of my peers were still trying to figure out their lives. While I was taking on business administration for Bayless, they were still jumping from dead-end job to dead-end job. It made it awkward to hang out much. Our lives were simply in different places. I found myself really missing my friends and the energy of New York. Kyle, who had become like a second brother to me, understood who I was and what I wanted from my life. But Kyle had stayed back in New York to follow his own path that would eventually lead him first to the New York Fed and later to working with state and local authorities to increase investment and opportunity for the inner-city communities of Detroit. We would stay in constant contact, but we were no longer on the same journey.

Feeling otherwise alone, I turned to my father for companionship.

This wasn't just a personal decision. If I was going to work with Dad, I needed to keep our relationship strong. His favorite thing to do outside work was to play golf, so almost immediately after I joined the business, I suggested I take up golfing with him and his friends.

Dad laughed at the very idea of it. I soon found out what was so funny. His closest friends were Frank Johnson and Eddie Johnson. I made up the last of four. Sometimes, Jason Kidd or some influential leader in the community joined us on the course. Other times, an Arizona Cardinals or Phoenix Suns veteran or two played.

Dad's friends were highly successful and *highly* competitive individuals. The way they played the game was a lot like friendly hazing—full of trash talk and escalating bets. I didn't have money to compete with multimillionaire ex-professional athletes, but that didn't stop them from stacking the bets—and the trash talk—against me anyway. Every game was like combat, and I was getting beat badly. Very badly.

I started taking lessons on the sly, hoping to improve enough to actually be competitive. Slowly but surely, I got better. But Dad's friends took my improvement as an opportunity to up the bets and the trash talking. In their version of "combat golf," every game was meant to escalate to all-out war—not just over who could make a birdie but who could throw out the most impressive insults. These guys had mastered the trash-talking trade at the highest level—and they were turning their considerable skill on me. They leveled taunts at me that took working for my dad as a starting point and spun out from there. I wasn't intimidated by their successes, but it took work to keep them from getting in my head.

In truth, I could handle the trash talking and the costs. What truly bothered me was the main topic of conversation. Since they were all former professional players, the focus was always on my brother. Everyone saw him as a success—maybe *the* success—and he was at the center of everything.

And that subject of conversation followed me well beyond the golf course to every place I went. If I met someone I knew on the sidewalk, they wanted to know about the points Jerryd scored in the last game. When I was at the gym to lift weights or play basketball, they wanted to hear if he was starting the next game. If I was asked about my work at all, it was always in terms of "your dad's business."

Thus, no matter where I was, I was always in someone's shadow. At the office, it was Dad's. On the golf course and in the gym, it was Jerryd's. There was no escaping it. No matter who I was talking to, everyone asked about Dad or Jerryd first. No one believed in or cared about my work at Bayless.

The shadow followed me home too. All our family vacations revolved around Jerryd's schedule. We planned holiday get-togethers around his games, which were the collective highlight of every gathering, and when we got together, the conversation was always about where he was traveling next.

I was trying to build a successful business that could help thousands of people in our community. I was on a path trying to create millions in wealth for myself, my family, and others in our business. I was also modeling the opportunity our community has to close the wealth gap through entrepreneurship.

But our society is so focused on sports and entertainment, it didn't matter what I was doing. My work at Bayless paled in comparison to a double-double in a prime-time NBA game.

All I could do was grit my teeth, take that chip on my shoulder, and use it to keep driving myself harder. As I have had time to reflect on this, many entrepreneurs start out in the shadow of a mentor, boss, or someone close to them. It is a natural process to develop and learn under someone who has accomplished something in their own right. I now realize that this was a blessing.

Even though, when I was young, that period was difficult, the head trash was fueling my inner fire to succeed.

The End of the Party

To really make the impact I wanted to, I'd have to make some tough choices and leave some opportunities behind. And that started with the one area where the attention was always on me. With my family, friends, and coworkers, I was always in someone else's shadow, but when I threw Red Carpet parties, I was at the center of things.

I soon found that there was still plenty of opportunity and need for parties. Jerryd asked me to start throwing parties for him, and I was happy to accommodate. Soon, I was throwing Red Carpet parties whether Jerryd was in town or not. Before I knew it, I was regularly promoting at a club in Scottsdale. And with Kyle back in New York, this time, the enterprise was all mine.

But the cumulative fatigue was catching up to me, and I was coming into the office drained. One day, right before Thanksgiving, I came into work after being out all night and fell asleep at my desk.

I startled awake to Dad cursing me out.

"If you want to party all night," he shouted, "go do that. If you want to come up with telemedicine solutions, this is the place—but make the choice."

He essentially said what Carla had a couple years before: *Are you going to throw parties or do you want to do this?* His words, like hers had, lit a fuse within me. And this time, I was ready to truly commit to one path.

I have always had a massive fear of failure that developed from my desire never to let my family down. Throughout school, college, and Wall Street, I was very conscious that my parents and the generations before us had sacrificed so much to give me these opportunities. I couldn't stand the idea of letting them down. I've used that fear to drive my work ethic. But in some ways, I already felt that I'd failed as a basketball player and at Red Carpet—both as the result of not putting in the effort. I decided I wouldn't fail at Bayless for lack of effort.

I closed down Red Carpet for good a few months later, and I went all in on Bayless.

Growth and Intuition

The first thing I did was move our company into growing our geriatric mental health services. I took the cumulative research Dad already had and homed in on skilled nursing facilities like the one I visited while considering my career options, trying to establish a precedent that would get more providers to follow suit. As we were putting together the vision, I commented that we would need to expand beyond this base. Already, an idea was forming in my mind. While it was all well and good to provide the mental health services necessary for geriatric care, I was intrigued by the integrated model used with long-term care within "dual eligible populations" (low-income individuals with both Medicaid and Medicare eligibility). Essentially, in an integrated care model, all mental and primary care was provided as a package. That's what they had at these skilled nursing facilities. Couldn't we expand that out to other populations? If it was seen as valuable to provide low-income elderly people with physical and mental health services in one location, why not provide that to everyone?

To make a dent in this space, though, we'd need help. Telehealth, integrated care—these were big, complex, ambitious ideas. I told Dad we needed experts in the field.

"I have the guy," Dad said. "I'll invite him to Phoenix for a meeting."

Dad called his old friend, Dr. Jon McCaine—the one who'd advised him to pursue me in the first place. Jon was working in

Tucson at the time. I met with him to tell him what I was working on and planning.

"I like it," he said. "Let's figure it out."

His ready acceptance of these ideas surprised me. I'd come to find many medical professionals younger than them skeptical of telehealth. But Jon and my dad shared a certain pragmatic streak. Both saw at once that this shift was inevitable and could allow for positive changes in treatment. Jon also had the additional experience of having worked in rural communities where patients struggled to get to an office. Being able to call in for mental health treatment from home would make a huge difference to those people.

Jon took the job with Bayless & Associates, where he would remain until I sold the company almost eleven years later. Once he joined in 2009, we worked together to simultaneously build two systems: our geriatric program and an intensive adolescent outpatient program to help teens transition into adulthood separate from the pediatrics department Dad had already established. While neither directly touched on telemedicine or integrated care, we felt we had to scale in both these directions first to create the space for those other programs to develop.

Jon was invaluable in these efforts. I call him the Zen Master. He was very similar to Dad in his approach to working with people—light on administration, heavy on relationships—but where Dad's strength was really in assessment, Jon was a master at behavioral planning intervention. He knew all the tools and techniques that could improve outcomes for patients without having to resort to pharmaceuticals. Like Dad, he was also extremely engaging with people, and his way with clinicians never failed to get them on board with our mission. His Zen approach allowed us to build followership early for everything that was to come.

With efforts for the geriatrics and adolescent programs underway by the spring of 2009, I turned my focus to Dad's dream of telehealth. Jon and I traveled to Las Vegas with our IT consultant for a conference given by the American Telemedicine Association at the Rio Hotel. Our goal was to learn two things. First, we needed a use case for telemedicine. Mental health providers were nervous about choosing the right clients to approve for telemedicine treatment, fearing that it could cause an adverse event in the wrong patient. We'd need to prove to them that this had widespread potential. Second, we needed to know more about technology and get an idea of the investment cost so we could begin work integrating telehealth into our business.

The conference took place in a small room with fewer than a couple hundred people—a sign that you might read optimistically as proof we were pioneers among health providers in this area. Less optimistically, you could argue it was a sign we'd arrived too early. I think it was probably a bit of both. We certainly learned technology was a hurdle. In 2009 the internet was slow, most people didn't have access to high-speed connections, and nothing was mobile. If we wanted to start offering this service, we'd need dedicated phone lines to provide reliable care. We'd also need at least six figures—a startup investment that was steep for us at the time.

Despite these reservations, about sixty days after the conference, we launched our beta program in a skilled nursing facility. We hired a coordinator between the facility and providers, and we were the first to do anything like that in our area.

I wish I could claim it was a success, but in reality, it was an absolute train wreck.

For starters, the facility's internet line continually had problems. We found out later that this was likely due to a nearby school. When classes were in the computer lab, their internet usage would suck up all the bandwidth in the area. That caused our telemedicine screens to freeze. That wasn't a good outcome for patients with mental health issues.

But it wasn't all bad news. Patients whose visits were not unencumbered by technological glitches showed a lot of improvement. They disclosed more information, and their providers noted that their sessions were more efficient.

There was clearly a lot of promise, but the margins weren't there. The necessary additional technological investment was out of our price range, and the sunk cost of what we'd already spent was becoming a black hole as we continued to invest in more technology to improve our internet connection. Ultimately, we had to put it on hold. That broke my dad's heart a bit, but I convinced him that we could make more profits by increasing the volume of services through the doctors we sent out to the facilities and growing more long-term and mental health services for adolescents while we waited for technology to catch up to our telehealth ambitions.

Over the next year, those long-term care efforts began to show fruit. We went from six employees in 2008 to forty and increased our profits. The medical outcomes were improving as well. People were having fewer return visits to the hospital and better outcomes. That made the insurance providers happy. Dad was initially suspicious, but as I put up wins, I won him over too.

Soon, we needed more space. In 2010, the long-term care department had greatly outgrown the office that contained all our administration, Dad's established pediatric mental healthcare, his forensic practice, and our new programs all in one building. Between the comings and goings of older patients, kids and their parents, teenagers, psychiatric providers, counselors, and our team of administrators, it was getting too busy to be comfortable.

We started actively looking for a second location. Eventually, we found an old Mexican steak house in South Mountain on the south side of Phoenix. The restaurant had gone bankrupt in the Great Recession. People were outside it using drugs and loitering. Again, I saw opportunity in an unlikely place. The location didn't look ideal now, but the community had only one other mental health facility in the surrounding area. Why not expand in an area with such a clear need for mental health services?

We prepared to acquire the South Mountain property and asked a state program, that I referred to as "the Network," for funding to develop it. They readily agreed. I hired a contractor, and we proceeded to title for the closing. Then, at the last minute, while Dad and I were literally sitting at the title company to sign the official paperwork, the Network sent an email. *Sorry,* it read. *After further review, we're unable to provide funding for your project due to limited financial resources.*

I showed the email to Dad just as he prepared to sign his name to the contracts for the new facility.

He looked straight at me. "What do you want to do?" he asked.

The South Mountain site could easily become a financial millstone around the company's neck without that funding. If we walked away from the deal, all we stood to lose was our earnest money. That was a persuasive argument for backing out, but more compelling was the intuition I couldn't shake.

"I think we're meant to do this," I said.

Dad nodded. He sat down at a table in the title company's office, and we signed the loan paperwork.

Thrown into Leadership

As I threw myself into the business of Bayless & Associates, the one thing I thought I had was time. I was supposed to take over in a decade. The business was small, but it was stable. Dad's forensic psychology seemed like a distraction to me, but it kept revenue coming in. I had years to get projects up and running successfully.

But that changed in an instant.

About two months after we closed on the new property, Dad had a heart attack. He had to be revived in the hospital and was in the ICU for two weeks. As he recovered, it became very clear he'd never be able to work again.

I immediately took over the entire business—but not without some extra complications. Because I didn't have a medical or clinical license, I couldn't legally run Bayless & Associates. So I had to scramble. I ran to the lawyer's office to change the company's name and incorporation status overnight. As soon as Dad was up and able, he signed off on the change from PC to incorporated, which would allow me to take over.

Dr. McCaine helped me a lot as Dad transitioned out of the business. And I needed his help—because now that I was in power, I had big plans I intended to implement. In those circumstances, most people would focus on stabilizing the company after taking such a blow. I chose to take a big risk instead.

The first thing I did was shut down the forensic practice.

Since his heart attack, Dad's protégé, Dr. Janeen DeMarte, had taken over his cases and had already made a name for herself at the Jodi Arias trial. She wanted to step up and keep things running, but I decided now was the moment for a clean break. My decision was partly driven by bitterness, partly by concern for Dad, and partly by practicality. The forensic practice had taken up so much of his life. It had taken his health as well. He ate poorly, smoked, and spent eight hours on the stand anytime he was needed. I didn't want that to be an option anymore.

But I also didn't like the business model, which was built on the reputation of the doctors we worked with. Plus, the legal system paid bills very slowly. The profits were good, but the cash flow was terrible. It was far too difficult to scale.

On a certain, basic level, you have to trust your instincts as an entrepreneur. I'd been brought up in this company. My mother had raised me with a keen business sense. I'd gone to

Wall Street a year before my peers. I knew I had the experience and understanding to make the big calls.

As I considered the direction of the business, I thought back to a key moment in my time at Morgan Stanley. I was in the room with Carla, sitting across from an executive team for a major fast-food corporation. They were raising $500 million. They were at the top of their profession. As they discussed their strategy and targets, I realized that these people were no smarter than me.

That was no guarantee my ideas would prove right, but it did show that I had the capability to make the kinds of big calls those executives made. So I made one.

I pulled the plug, and a million-dollar revenue business at the time—two-thirds of our entire revenue, all built on my dad's name and reputation—went away overnight.

By the time we opened the South Mountain site in January 2011, I was president of a company fully focused on providing mental health services to the community. And I was cut out for the work ahead of me. With Dad retired, no forensic practice, and telehealth shelved, I had to find a way to grow the company.

Everything seemed to be against my taking this shot, but with that big chip on my shoulder, I decided I was going to take it anyway. To make that shot, though, I'd have to fight to change the whole Arizona medical system.

5

DAVID AND GOLIATH

With a lot of ambition and a whole company to run, it would have been easy to become overwhelmed. Part of the reason I was able to adapt quickly was due to the routines I had established in my life.

I was lucky enough to grow up in a family focused on routine. Mom, Dad, Jerryd—we all took care to set up regimens that would allow us to accomplish our ambitions while taking care of ourselves. Early on in my career, I'd learned the value of setting aside time for working out and healthy eating. I made sure, whatever else was going on, that I got enough sleep.

I'd also picked up from Carla the routine of always being the first in and the last out.

Such routines come at a certain price. There were times I had to pass on fun nights out with friends in order to ensure I got enough shut-eye. It wasn't always fun dragging myself to the gym when I was already tired and stressed out.

But these routines served me well because they meant I didn't burn out under the new pressure I was under. Instead, I had the energy and focus available to take on the challenges ahead.

And those challenges were certain to prove monumental.

It all started with my efforts to transition our community-based clinic into a Federally Qualified Health Center (FQHC). Organizations with FQHC status used a payment system that was better designed and could more easily allow companies to scale. The same month I opened South Mountain, I reached out to an FQHC in South Phoenix. Dad was skeptical, but against his wishes, I shadowed them for two weeks.

During that time, I observed clinic–patient interactions across multiple departments—family, pediatrics, OB-GYN, internal medicine. One day I found myself in a pediatrics exam room with a Black woman, her two sons, and a pediatrician who looked like Mr. Clean.

Their mother had made the appointment for her younger son, who was ten, because he was still wetting the bed. He was also on his last warning at school.

When we entered, the two boys were fighting—and practically destroying the room while they were at it.

"His dad's in jail. I'm at my wits' end," his mom said over the ruckus. "We're barely making ends meet, and something's wrong. I don't know what it is, but I know he needs help."

"You came to the right place," the doctor encouraged her. "We'll get to the bottom of this."

He mentioned that the clinic had a partner around the corner at Bayless that could help with her son's issues. She was visibly relieved when the doctor mentioned that he would send in a consultant after her son's exam to ask some questions. Soon Bridgette, a Hispanic woman, entered the room.

"I'm so sorry to hear all this," she said. She continued to speak with the boy's mother, her demeanor compassionate and kind. The boy's mom broke down in tears, her face in her hands. Bridgette said that she would get a referral for her son to Bayless. She also explained that a case worker would need to "rubber-stamp" the referral.

Back in 2010, so much legal red tape separated behavioral healthcare from primary healthcare that primary care couldn't refer directly to us. Because of that system, intermediaries embedded case managers who checked if care was "adequate" before sending the case over to mental health facilities.

In the middle of their discussion, the White woman assigned as the case manager on behalf of the Network entered the room.

"I'm here to schedule your son's psychiatric evaluation at Bayless," she said brusquely. The atmosphere in the room changed instantly. This indifferent woman set the mother on edge. Where everyone else had spoken from a place of understanding and compassion, that bureaucratic apathy must have connected to a thousand moments of dismissal throughout her life. And Mom reacted reflexively.

"My baby is *not* crazy," she shouted. "I didn't come here for this."

She stormed out of the room.

The case manager shrugged. She didn't seem to care that she'd probably ruined that boy's chance at getting behavioral healthcare. She told everyone left in the room she'd send over the referral later that day and went back to her office as if nothing had happened.

The next day, I shadowed an Asian American doctor within internal medicine. We entered an exam room to find a Hispanic family: a senior gentleman, his wife, and two younger adults who I assumed were his children. They were clinging to their elderly father while his wife stood nearby, seemingly holding him in place. He appeared to be in extreme mental distress, his eyes moving everywhere.

The doctor took in the scene, recognized the man's mental distress, and forewent the usual exam to immediately call Bridgette. She spoke Spanish to the man's wife before explaining the rubber-stamp referral policy in English to his kids.

Sadly, what came next played out the same as it had the day before. The Network case manager came in, used the words "psychiatric evaluation," and the family stormed out.

In the midst of that tragedy, a light bulb went off for me. Where previously integrated care had made sense on a logical level to me, I now truly *felt* the need to change the system. *This* was the real value of quality integrated care. If there was one less step in the process, both of those families would have received the care they needed. If we could bring primary and mental health services under one roof, Bayless could provide that care. But if I was going to make a difference, I'd have to bring the integrated care model online and prove it could work.

The Potential of Integrated Care

Coming out of that clinic, my mind buzzing with ideas, I knew there had to be a way to change things. In fact, for the first time in my life, I *knew* I had to take the lead on that change.

Entrepreneurs have to rely on their gut instincts quite often. What you're doing is unproven—until you prove it—so you have to trust your intuition. I'd always done this up to that point when I'd closed down the forensic practice, but I'd never felt completely sure of my decisions, until now.

I was so sure of my instincts that I heard a voice in the back of my head telling me that this was going to work. This was going to be the direction I took the company, and it was going to be a huge success. When I say there was a voice, I mean a real voice in this case. I don't know if that's rare or common with entrepreneurs, but I know that many have a moment when the path ahead takes on a kind of crystal clarity. That's what I was experiencing.

Some people call this a calling. I'm not particularly religious, but I did feel a connection to something. I have a sense that everyone has a voice like this, it's just most people don't listen to it.

I was going to listen to mine.

But I also knew that listening wasn't going to make the way forward any easier. I was up against a very broken system. This was right before the Affordable Care Act (ACA) expanded access to mental healthcare, and the unvarnished truth was that people weren't getting access to the services they so desperately needed. Despite some progress after that law passed, this is still unfortunately a massive issue that has been plaguing the country.

According to the CDC, one in five Americans has a diagnosable mental health condition at any one time, and 40 percent have reported symptoms of depression or anxiety.[1] For all that clear need, our system simply lacks the ability to help our people. The American Psychological Association has found that 65 percent of psychologists have no capacity for new patients.[2] That means more than half of people who need mental healthcare don't receive it. For minority communities and lower-income communities, that number is even worse—especially for kids.

For Black and Brown children and adults, it can be extremely difficult to find someone from their communities to provide care. According, once again, to the American Psychological Association, only 15 percent of psychologists are non-White.[3] For families like those I saw at that FQHC, that means they are often unable to see someone whom they feel comfortable opening up to and that has the cultural competency to provide the support they need—if they can see anyone at all.

The only bit of luck we have going for us is that our society is slowly coming to realize the scope of this problem and our need to address it. When I was growing up there was a real stigma about going to see a therapist. Thankfully, that is starting to disappear, and people speak far more openly about their mental health issues these days. However, talk isn't enough. As a nation we need to create more access for people to receive the care they need—and at the *time* they need it.

Getting help with mental health isn't like going to the emergency room after tearing your ACL. Most people seeking mental health assistance urgently require immediate attention, in the same way a person who goes to the ER for a serious injury does—they have a situation, and they need a resolution. They need to see someone, and they need to see them *now*.

Unfortunately, because of the lack of capacity, it can take months to get an appointment—and the timeline compounds the problem. Imagine if you had to wait three days every time you needed to go to the ER, and you get an idea of the severity of the problem. Under those circumstances, people do the only thing they can: find a way to cope as best they can. Once a person has lived with the problem for a day or two, they begin to think they can handle it on their own. Sadly, they often "handle it" by turning to drugs, alcohol, and other unhealthy behaviors.

As I thought about these complex issues after visiting the FQHC, the scope of my mission expanded. I realized that if I could help get people into care within seventy-two hours of the time they requested it, it could change everything.

That realization was the pivotal moment in my career: Suddenly, I knew how to change the system. Integrated healthcare had to do away with the old separations that existed in psychiatric care, make mental healthcare mirror medical healthcare, and provide the same kind of access to behavioral health services as urgent care does. If we could pull that off, we could scale that care and normalize it the same way we expect care for broken bones and torn ACLs.

A huge part of this shift would depend on something I learned while observing treatment at the FQHC: Most people will trust their doctor when they have something going on that's related to mental health. This is why both patients I saw were comfortable admitting their issues to their doctor when they came in. It was only when the health plan bureaucrats got involved that the link between primary and mental healthcare broke down. If that doctor could provide their patient a "warm handoff"—transferring care in front of the patient—to a mental health professional who would work directly with them on the same day, I knew the actual chance that the patient would follow through with care would expand exponentially.

In the years to come, my hunch was proven right. Before these changes, our rate of no-show appointments would average 30 to 40 percent. Once we began using this integrated care model with virtual availability, that rate fell below 11 percent. Ultimately, this system would give patients opportunities to stay out of higher levels of care and address the underlying issues that had been plaguing their families *before* drugs and other tragic results occurred.

But before we could get to that point, I had a number of battles to fight, and the first one up was convincing Dad that this could work.

After my epiphany I drove over to see him and discuss my plan. Dad agreed to listen to my pitch, but he demonstrated his skepticism by taking the "meeting" in his bathrobe.

"Here's what we need to do," I said, and proceeded to explain the vision as far as I'd sketched it out.

When I finished, he cursed me out.

"Medical and behavioral are oil and water," he shouted. "They've never gotten along. They tried it back in the '80s, and it failed. Stop wasting my retirement and get things back to how they were."

I hadn't even used the words *integrated care*. But after decades of working in the system—with all its challenges and limitations—Dad was more than a little reluctant. He might have even been convinced that kind of change was impossible.

I always took my father's feedback very seriously. I respected him more than anyone else in the world. But I knew I was onto something. So I stood up to him and challenged his dismissal of the idea.

We went back and forth on it until Dad finally waved his objections away.

"Fine," he said. "Show me a business plan."

A Corrupt and Complex System

Dad wasn't being needlessly obstinate. He knew just how hard it would be to introduce this kind of restructuring in the medical system. The change I proposed might seem like an obvious one, but it was incredibly difficult to pull off.

To understand why, you have to understand how mental healthcare worked in Arizona. For a very long time—decades in fact—mental healthcare was an afterthought for the state. It wasn't just a low priority; it wasn't a mainstream priority at all. Then, in early 2011, a man with mental health issues shot Congresswoman Gabby Giffords in Tucson, shocking the country and the system. For the first time, mental health issues very publicly and directly impacted the government. Overnight, mental health changed from a nonissue to something that needed to be dealt with. The conversation was everywhere.

But conversations didn't remove the structural obstacles in the way of better treatment. It didn't change the need for the "rubber stamp" or the biases plaguing the system. Even now, mental health guidelines haven't changed much since the 1960s. Mental health professionals are trained to work in different environments than primary care. There are requirements for one-hour appointments and conflict-of-interest issues that prevent a mental health professional from treating anyone they know, even though there are no corresponding restrictions on medical physicians.

And these weren't the only roadblocks by any means. In the integrated setting I envisioned, communication between mental health and medical care providers would be extremely important. But because of antiquated rules and protections around mental health and substance abuse data, these same providers couldn't share information even with each other about their mutual patients without certain types of consent. Those same "protections" also prevented practitioners from the medical and behavioral sides from working within the same technological platforms.

In other words, my goal of an integrative, community-focused delivery system was a direct challenge to the status quo of the entire American mental healthcare system and numerous Arizona standards and practices. So before we could even dream of scaling integrated care, we had to create a system and infrastructure in which a psychiatrist and a primary care physician could work side by side and share information so they could deliver meaningful care to our patients.

And we had to find a way to get paid for it. That proved the most frustrating and uncompromising obstacle of all.

Back when I was dreaming this idea up, the mental health insurance benefits structure was completely separated from primary care. For example, insurance payers would not allow medical and behavioral providers under the same roof to bill certain codes on the same day. This was simply because the psychiatrist and medical doctor were in the same building. If a patient walked across the street to see another provider, there wouldn't be a problem. No limitations for that kind of billing existed.

Since we didn't want to rely on the financial responsibility of people in mental health crises, this represented an existential issue to the company. We needed to figure out how insurance could cover care. That would ensure people didn't have a high out-of-pocket cost and we had a dependable payment system. It was the only way to build a sustainable business capable of continuing care.

To solve this, I'd have to take on the true Goliath in the room: Arizona's Medicaid funding system. When we got started, Arizona was one of the most funded states in America for mental health, but according to the Mental Health America, as recently as 2022, it had the second-worst outcomes for providing care.[4] The underlying issue was that over time, the Arizona mental healthcare system had been corrupted by intermediary groups embedded within it. These groups were originally meant to act as watchdogs, ensuring care was delivered and funding was appropriately allocated, but the opposite happened. Bureaucracy, large overheads, and corporate greed resulted in ineffective care, and these intermediaries became more invested in maintaining the status quo than delivering better care.

To understand how these intermediary groups came into power in Arizona, you have to understand the health-care payer system in America. Healthcare in America is delivered by three separate payer services: Medicare, which provides federal dollars for older adults; Medicaid, which is state funded, for low-income individuals; and commercial insurance, which is provided by employers to employees or is purchased directly by individuals through the marketplace established by the ACA.

Medicare recognizes only a small sliver of mental healthcare providers. Within mental healthcare, it will only reimburse services by a licensed clinical social worker, psychologist, or psychiatrist. This creates absurd gaps in coverage. For instance, until late 2022 Medicare did not recognize professional counselors or marriage counselors. Congress has been slow to update these laws for decades. In other words, Medicare would limit what mental health practitioners we could use if we tried to integrate care—an extra hurdle we didn't need.

Amazingly, the commercial insurance payer system has traditionally been even worse. Until the ACA, most insurers didn't believe in covering behavioral health at all. When I suggested integrated care to the chief medical officer (CMO) of one of the largest publicly traded insurance companies, he laughed, dismissed the idea, and left the meeting after five minutes. He and others demonstrated no interest whatsoever in delivering quality mental healthcare to the population. So while in theory integrated care would have been easier with commercial insurance, we had no potential partners.

That left Medicaid. Medicaid is delivered by government organizations set up by each state. It's also the big fish in mental health. Medicaid is the number one payer for mental health in the country. In Arizona, it was also where I found a willing partner. Arizona Health Care Cost Containment System, or AHCCCS, is Arizona's Medicaid system. I've always seen AHCCCS as an ally. As we'll see in the chapters ahead, they were supportive of my efforts long before others in the industry were won over.

In theory, this support should have been enough to clear a path for integrated care in Arizona. After all, AHCCCS provides oversight of the managed care companies that deliver care to the population. Unfortunately, that was mostly just theory.

By the time I was on the scene, AHCCCS's oversight role was little more than hypothetical for mental healthcare. Arizona had become notoriously inept at ensuring the delivery of mental healthcare, and the state had subsequently farmed out the management of mental health to the Arizona Department of Health Services (ADHS), an entirely different state agency—and one extremely skeptical of just about every idea I had to improve the system.

To provide its oversight, ADHS named a company to act as the Regional Behavioral Health Authority, or RBHA. The RBHA functioned much in the same way as an insurance company while managing the companies that delivered mental healthcare.

Within this system, the designated RBHA company awarded intermediary entities contracts to deliver mental healthcare. These contracts, or "block grants," were another huge issue within the Arizona system. Recipients of block grants were allowed to provide care *up to the amount of the grant*, but there was no more money if they went over that amount. And if they billed less than that amount, say $450,000 on a $500,000 grant, for any reason—even because patients had improved and didn't need as much care—the clinic had to pay back the remaining $50,000. They were then likely to receive less funding the following year.

The block grant system incentivized providers to provide the cheapest level of care to make sure they could always get the maximum renewal amount. It didn't incentivize them to hire more expensive licensed professionals. Instead, it incentivized "care management"—technician-level care that requires minimal training and doesn't require an advanced degree.

If your head hurts reading all that, imagine trying to not only understand this system but improve it.

All of this is to say, Dad was probably right. It was a crazy idea to shake the hornet's nest and try to take on this convoluted, corrupt system. But I wasn't going to let that stop me.

Standing Out Again

The difficulties ahead weren't just systemic—and they weren't just related to care. As I began my battle for integrated care, I found that the rooms I was entering usually only admitted certain types of people who made certain type of assumptions.

These rooms were filled with social workers for the most part—not businesspeople—who had worked their way up to the C-suite. Most of them were White. Other than me, there were maybe one or two minority leaders in the mental health system in Arizona. Otherwise, there was no one in the leadership who came from different communities or could represent the interests of those who most needed care. Predictably, they treated the system accordingly, as if the only thing to do was accept it and work within its constraints.

Symptomatic of this lack of diversity was the system's audits for "cultural competency" that included a lot of box-ticking without any practical value. This led to some absurd situations.

For instance, despite our entire office at Bayless being bilingual and multiethnic, the powers that be tried to cite us for not having adequate signage that was translated into Spanish. It was just part of the infuriating but prevailing disconnect between objectives and organization. On more than one occasion, I angrily dismissed those audits—and the auditors—by demanding they show me another clinic in the valley with as much ethnic, religious, and cultural competency as ours.

Dad understood all that. For many years, he had been the only Black person in the room. He had been vocal about how the system was hurting communities, specifically communities of color, and preventing them from moving beyond their legacies of intergenerational trauma. I'm sure that's why he was so hard on my ideas at first.

And perhaps that's why he let himself be won over by my vision.

I presented my business plan to him in the weeks after the Gabby Giffords shooting. Still outwardly skeptical, Dad met me in his robe again. I closed my pitch with an appeal.

"You challenged me to come and help the business," I said. "You call yourself a clinician. You're supposed to be a healer. I'm trying to help more people so the stuff we see on TV doesn't happen anymore."

Of course, he pushed back.

"What am I here for if not for this?" I demanded. "This is our opportunity to do something different. If you don't want to do this, then *why am I here?*"

It worked. Dad called the next day and greenlit the initiative.

His support wasn't just sentimental. I had the facts on my side. Combining mental and physical health was the best way to provide health, and ultimately it could save costs. As a government agency, Medicaid's duty was to make sure that dollars were placed in the best hands to provide the best services at the lowest cost. That's what managed care is all about. All I had to do was prove integrated care could lead to better outcomes at a lower cost.

Easier said than done, of course.

The first challenge was even getting a hearing on these ideas. Bayless was not a top twelve provider in the RBHA Network entity at the time. My dad had been kept in the system as one of the only minority-owned providers, but he had never been offered a seat on the board.

To move things forward, I had to scream louder than anyone else. I agitated for more funding by demanding transparency within the industry so I could prove that our outcomes were better than everyone else's. As we started sharing those better outcomes, I asked for larger and larger block grants to facilitate our growth. When the Network said they didn't have any more funding to give me, I'd run the publicly available numbers to show that they did.

In my quest for more funding to grow our practice, I got a reputation as a troublemaker. I was always pushing people to change systems, always insisting—loudly—that block grants were terrible.

The harder I pressed the people in control, the harder they pressed back. When I suggested that failing to fund these changes would lead to the whole system coming down around them, I got laughed out of the room—again. But I didn't give up, and I certainly didn't fall in line. Instead, I began to attack the system locally by pointing out where the Network intermediaries weren't following state guidelines. Putting my accounting degree to work, I showed how much these issues were costing taxpayers. The more I questioned where the money was going—and why the outcomes weren't improving—the more attention I garnered from both sides of the political aisle.

I may have been a troublemaker, but I was a relentless one. I showed everyone in the system I was up for a fight—and I was determined to win.

Growing through Adversity

Considering the difficulties ahead, you might be wondering why I didn't just choose an easier path. After all, other mental health organizations had worked within the broken system and found success; why couldn't I calm down and carve out my niche? Why put everything into this fight?

Beyond the obvious point that I knew the system was broken, the plain truth is that I was addicted to the fight. I still had that chip on my shoulder, and I was determined to prove I could not just succeed but excel. In this sense, I was like most entrepreneurs—who struggle with a form of addiction, whether they realize it or not. Entrepreneurs live for the adrenaline of getting into the room and proving to everyone that they were right. They're fueled by people saying no to them. They live for the highs and can barely stand the lows.

That addiction gives them the benefits of extreme motivation that can help push through the tough times ahead. But there are downsides, some of which we'll see ahead. Entrepreneurship on this level takes a toll. It can ruin your health and break relationships. Looking back, I suspect one of the reasons my parents split up was that Dad was so focused on the business, he chronically undervalued Mom.

As I set my sights on this massive, systemic challenge, that was the level of sacrifice I might be called to make. I had to be willing to put almost everything into the company—and put what was left in the parts of my life I wanted to hold on to. Nothing else was going to be enough.

Effort always wasn't going to be enough—not in and of itself. I had to get creative to find a way forward. To win this fight, we were going to have to grow the business enough to demonstrate those better outcomes at scale. But growth was a particularly difficult challenge. To grow, we needed larger block grants. Regardless of how much I fought, the block grants weren't coming unless we could demonstrate better outcomes. It was a vicious cycle.

Lacking further block grants, I had no choice but to borrow the capital to expand. In spring 2011, I closed on a $3 million SBA loan from JPMorgan Chase. I took $500,000 of it and closed our main office for seven months to renovate and prepare for an integrated health relaunch. I also opened a separate administrative office.

Most of the rest I used to keep the company going while we survived on the revenue coming from the South Mountain office. Keep in mind that I had also shuttered our main source of income: the forensic practice. In other words, in a very short period of time, I had placed limits on our earnings potential and taken on an immense amount of debt to expand under a totally unproven concept. It was high risk to say the least.

I also placed one final bet with that $3 million loan. I put $750,000 of it into qualifying as an FQHC like the location I'd shadowed. Their funding method was very different from the block grant system that Bayless & Associates relied on, and I thought it could provide us a work-around. Once qualified, we would be reimbursed the investment I put into the effort.

But it didn't work out as I'd hoped. Although the FQHC reviewers from Washington, DC, recognized that we had the need within our community and that we met most of the requirements, we were declined. In this case, we were simply unlucky. We were the first organization reviewed under newer, stricter guidelines put in place because other companies had been caught abusing the system. We checked all the original boxes, but the government had decided to take a more skeptical view of organizations shifting into FQHC status.

Dad was in the room when they told us we weren't approved. I remember looking at him and just walking out. It was one of the hardest days of my life. I went to the driving range and hit golf balls for five hours, until my hands were bloody, blistered, and raw. We had lost all the money and time invested in the process and were at significant risk of bankruptcy.

Afterward, Dad called. He told me not to beat myself up. I'd followed the best path I could. He may not have initially believed in that path, but now that he'd signed up, he was all in. He'd continue to be my best ally in the coming fight.

In the aftermath of that failure, I didn't take a salary for almost a year. I sold my car and borrowed my dad's second car—a 1996 Land Cruiser with 200,000 miles that Jerryd had wrecked years before. Everyone, including me, called that car the "Green Bomber."

We were in dire straits. And things were about to get even harder.

6

DOUBLE RAINBOW

Despite setbacks, I refused to slow down. In fact, I continued to double down. Such resilience is necessary in entrepreneurship. The path I was on required an understanding and acceptance of sacrifice. It was a lesson I learned from my father, a man who had spent long hours at work just to keep the office running. There are only so many hours, so much attention, so much energy we have in a day, and he put a lot of that toward Bayless. That's the reason most of my childhood memories of him involved being in his office.

I'd already made my share of sacrifices at that point. I'd sacrificed going out at Morehouse to get an early start on my career. While others were partying in their final semester, I was already working full time on the Street. Selling my car and going without a salary was just part of the price I'd have to pay if I wanted to be a success. And I wasn't about to let that slow me down.

One of my first acts of doubling down was to focus on our brand. A company's brand deserves attention and care. Your brand is a reflection of who you are. Its value is nearly priceless. And it was time for Bayless to rebrand.

This was another lesson I first learned from Dad. He'd named his company after himself, calling it Michael B. Bayless

& Associates. The name was stuffy on purpose. He was his company's main asset, and his clients were all lawyers who loved a good, stuffy business name.

But that was now a thing of the past. It was time to come up with a name and an image that spoke to our new vision.

So, in 2012, I hired a consultant to spend a year with the team and come up with a name and image that would allow us to rebrand the company. With their help, we developed the image that would come to symbolize Bayless and everything we were doing: the butterfly with a human face in its wing.

Bayless Integrated Healthcare South Mountain Clinic

I'd been inspired by the idea of transformation symbolized by the butterfly. It always brought an old Buckminster Fuller quote to mind: "There is nothing in a caterpillar that tells you it's going to be a butterfly." That's the message we wanted to get across to our patients. They may not feel like they could become butterflies when they walked in, but that butterfly existed within them.

And the same was true of Bayless. The organization may not yet seem like it could change the system and prove a success, but those elements already existed within it. One day, I knew it would spread its wings and fly.

We had the new Bayless logo just in time to reopen our main office, now branded with our new name: Bayless Integrated Healthcare.

Our expansion went even further in 2013 when I decided to use the remainder of the loan funding to acquire Rainbow Pediatrics. Acquiring Rainbow was an attractive prospect for several reasons. Most significantly, it was a sizable practice, with eight thousand pediatric patients. Such a huge sample would certainly help us prove out our thesis of integrated care. At the same time, most of those patients—around five thousand in total—were on Medicaid. The sheer size of our patient load would allow us to put pressure on the RBHA Network and push them to fully pay for mental health services, especially since we could demonstrate that the level of mental healthcare for these children fell well below the accepted industry prevalence standards.

Back then, the payer system was extremely opaque, and that meant the Medicaid agency's data wasn't very good. But we knew generalized prevalence rates in Medicaid populations stated that 30 to 40 percent of Medicaid children have an underlying mental health disorder due to the strain that poverty places on their lives. One in five has a diagnosable mental health disorder.[5]

When we looked at Rainbow's numbers, they told a pretty damning story. Out of the five thousand Medicaid children who were patients there, only two hundred of them had ever been enrolled in the RBHA for mental healthcare. Given the prevalence rates, that number should have been closer to two thousand. The needs of these kids simply weren't being met.

We acquired Rainbow Pediatrics in July 2013 and began integrating services. By that October, we were serving 1,200 of those five thousand patients—essentially ensuring one thousand more kids who needed mental health services were getting care. It was a huge win, but of course, it wasn't that simple.

When we purchased Rainbow we paid in cash using the loan funding, gave the doctor a nice salary, kept his team in place, and saw about a 550 percent increase in patients receiving mental healthcare. The increase alone should have meant Bayless received more block grant funding, but we didn't get a single extra dollar. Instead, while the pediatric side of the business increased our revenue, we were paying out of pocket to cover the services for these kids because the Network and the RBHA simply . . . wouldn't.

I was prepared and determined to bring the fight to the public behavioral health system, but costs were stacking up. We were already bleeding cash. And we were still trapped in the same vicious cycle. We couldn't scale integrated health for children without more funding, but we couldn't get more funding until we could prove it would scale. Stress piled on alongside the debt.

I'd stopped taking a salary. I'd sold my car. But we were still short. And I didn't know how we were going to pay for everything.

Happiness and Disappointment

At least by that point I had Jamil McCloud, my future wife, in my life—although she hadn't made it easy on me to get that first date.

I met her one night in July, around the same time I closed on Rainbow Pediatrics. She was out with her fellow nurses for a bachelorette party. After I introduced myself to her, she asked me what I did for a living.

Feeling a little self-conscious about the state of the business, I answered, "I'm a health-care administrator."

Jamil was understandably skeptical. "Okay, that seems super vague. What does that mean?"

I tried a more direct approach. "I'm the CEO of a company that provides integrated care."

"You're full of it," she said.

"No, it's true. Look." I pulled a card from my wallet and handed it over.

She took it, but she still walked away.

I couldn't blame her. Jamil was a beautiful woman, and she'd had more than her share of men claiming all kinds of impressive credentials to get her attention. How likely was it that this young guy who approached her out of nowhere was actually a CEO trying to change healthcare? Not that she would have cared either way, but the bold claim definitely seemed a bit suspect.

But she did keep my card.

I didn't let much time pass before I found her on Facebook. I sent a message saying it was nice to meet her and that I'd love to get together. She told me she wasn't interested. Her guard was up, and she was determined to ignore my romantic advances. But she didn't close the door entirely. She asked if we could network. I agreed, but when we met for coffee I told her I'd lied. I wasn't interested in networking. I was interested in her.

Surprisingly, that single-mindedness won her over. Something in how I laid my heart on my sleeve convinced her I might be legit and worth giving a chance. She told me later she had been impressed by my resiliency. And that was that.

Or *almost* that. Before I was allowed to take Jamil on a date, I had to meet her friends. I obligingly drove the Green Bomber to one of their apartments, where the three of them gave me a respectable grilling. I passed the test, and Jamil finally let me take her out.

Jamil brought a lot to my life. She calmed me and allowed me to settle down and focus. I honestly became a better person because she was in my life. And her belief was invaluable. She believed in my vision and what I was trying to accomplish—which was a rare quality at certain periods. She appreciated my idealism and my unflinching approach to the challenges I faced. While the rest of the world was indifferent or antagonistic, I now had someone who was a fellow believer and truly on my side.

She also had a similar type of bulldogged single-mindedness. Once she knew what she wanted, she would do whatever it took to achieve it. There's no limit to the value of having someone like that in your corner.

There was a further benefit to having her in my life: her family. After we'd been together for a few months, I went to meet them over the 2013 holidays in Vancouver, Washington, a town across the river from Portland, Oregon, where her uncle, Craig Bowen, hosted the entire family at his house. For the first time, I experienced a family that didn't take every opportunity to go out or distract themselves. Jamil's family just stayed in and enjoyed spending time together. They played games, drank wine, ate together, and created a warm, loving environment. I quickly fell into a natural alignment with them.

Jamil's family became a wealth of support and experience for me. They understood what I was trying to do with Bayless on a deep level. Jamil herself was a nurse who had originally been a business major (only switching majors because she felt nursing connected more directly to her nurturing, compassionate nature). Both medicine and business were interests she came by naturally. Dr. Dale Bowen, Jamil's grandfather, was a physician for over forty years and later became the director of integrated health services at Arizona State. Craig and his wife, Esther, were entrepreneurs. They founded GiftTree, a gift basket company that competes with Harry & David. Jamil's mother, Debbie, was an entrepreneur and inventor in her own right. She created the reusable diaper, which was sold at Nordstrom, Dillard's, and Neiman Marcus. That would be enough for most people, but Debbie went on to found a tech company that helped car companies show tire customization online, before going on to become one of the top five mortgage bankers in the country. Impressive doesn't begin to describe her.

Debbie has continued to be an important presence in my life, but at that holiday gathering, it was Craig who really took me under his wing. Craig is one of the most visionary individuals I've ever met and was the first to crack Google's pay-per-click algorithm. He also happens to be a great listener. I told him about the things I was going through at Bayless—bringing different forms of healthcare together and the stress of fighting the system. Craig had actionable insights I could use. He taught me the value of operational efficiency—which unlocked the growth dilemma I'd been struggling with.

Craig helped me realize there were ways to free up money without freeing up funding through the RBHA. With greater operational efficiency, we could improve our profitability even without a larger block grant. Before I left, he handed me a book by Gino Wickman called *Traction*, about the Entrepreneurial Operating System, or EOS for short.

That book, and Craig's guidance, sent me on a journey that would change how I ran my entire business. I learned about the value of creating systems that would allow everyone in the company to speak the same language. I found templates that helped clarify expectations and create accountability across positions. For the first time, I could chart who was a great fit for the company and deserved a promotion versus those who were a poor fit. And there was so much I didn't know about meetings: how often to meet, what to cover in a meeting, what to cover elsewhere.

It was a one-stop course in business management—the sort I missed out on by skipping the MBA when I went straight into entrepreneurship.

One of the greatest lessons from that period came not from EOS itself but from trying to implement it on my own. I spent months attempting to install new systems across the company. Eventually, I hit a wall. It was the first time I realized that I couldn't run this company on my own. I had to release a little control and delegate some responsibility.

With a little searching, I found the perfect person, an EOS implementer named Michael Erath, who proved that value of putting my trust in talented, experienced people.

Around the same time, I brought on another experienced hand, Arthur Pelberg, who began consulting with our practice. I'd met Arthur the year before, and we'd connected on a shared interest in integrated care. Now, we were working together to solve the massive obstacles in our way.

I entered 2014 with life and the company in a far better place. I had installed the entrepreneurial operating system and was seeing some early improvements. Dad, recognizing my progress, decided it was time to step away from the company more fully. He'd remained in the background after his heart attack but now felt he could safely leave me in full control of the organization.

With renewed confidence, I prepared for another ambitious effort to improve our funding. This time, I had an in. Arthur was one of the former partners of Schaller Anderson. They sold the company to Aetna Medicaid, but most of his people were still in place and were managing the company that had become the new RBHA, and therefore dispensed the Medicaid funds we needed. We assumed that meant we'd get a fair hearing when we asked for more funding to cover the new patients we were providing with services.

It didn't work out that way.

The people at the new RBHA *did* give us a fair hearing. They even agreed with our vision. But they didn't get to make the final decision.

The bureaucracy of the system was such that the call was out of Arthur's former team's hands. Instead, the decision went to an organization staffed mostly with the same people who had had the last RBHA contract with the state. The new CEO responsible for the RBHA wasn't willing to rock the boat by taking a chance on integrated care. Basically, it was a new name on the same adversary who'd caused us problems before.

I should have known better. After all, Arthur had warned me. When we had met a year before, he asked me, "How big of a Kevlar vest do you have?"

I didn't understand at first, so he explained, "You're trying to change the whole medical system, and everyone is going to be shooting at you."

As news of our setback came in, problems boiled over with the founder of Rainbow Pediatrics.

He had never been a good culture fit for our company—he'd alienated many of our primary care physicians and providers and upset a number of our psychiatrists and nurse practitioners. But now, he was beginning to spiral. What little faith he had in the vision for integrated care had been lost. Meanwhile, he had filed for bankruptcy, and he expected Bayless to bail him out—even as he was failing to meet his contractual obligations.

I couldn't focus my attention on his complaints. In September 2014, when our finances couldn't get any tighter, a one-hundred-year storm rolled through Phoenix and flooded the main office. Closing our doors for even one day could have put us out of business at that point, so the team and I stayed up all night with a company we'd hired to pump out the water. Miraculously, not a single patient's care was disrupted.

But the ordeal was clearly the last straw for the doctor at Rainbow.

A month later, in a midnight move, he took his files, opened a place across the street, and told the payers that all those patients belonged to his new practice. After all the work—all the investment—we were left with a hollowed-out center with no patients and no chief pediatrician. I filed a lawsuit against the doctor for stealing our patients, but I wasn't hopeful for a positive resolution. Before that, I hadn't thought the hole we were in could get any deeper.

His departure was a serious gut check, and it was tempting to give up on the idea of integrated care all together. But I resolved to keep moving forward. Staffing costs were a financial strain, but I chose not to let any team members go. I simply didn't believe in laying people off when things got tough. I hadn't dropped anyone during the Great Recession, and I wasn't about to start. The staff was grateful, and the culture improved, but I began to feel the stress personally.

One morning, Jamil was over at my home when I suddenly passed out. When I came to, she was there trying to figure out what was happening. And then I passed out again.

I thought I might be dying. I went to the hospital and went through several rounds of medical exams. After a tense wait, the diagnosis that came back was unanimous: my body was caving to stress, and if I didn't find a way to heal it, things weren't going to improve.

Unfortunately, I had no good options in front of me. None of my plans to increase revenue had worked out. We were bootstrapping like crazy to keep going, and things were bad. There seemed to be no foreseeable end to the downturn.

Dad's Dream

Then, a lifeline. In December 2014, the *Arizona Republic* published a series of articles on its front page. The headline takeaway was the immense corruption of the Arizona Medicaid system. For five days straight, investigative reporter Craig Harris detailed all the questionable practices in how the RBHA was handing out block grants. That got the attention of AHCCCS. For the first time in my career, I saw the wheels of change start to turn on that creaky institution.

To take advantage of the opportunity, I knew I had to make some major changes.

Among the big ideas Craig Bowen had introduced me to was vertical integration and the value of bringing outsourced services in-house. In healthcare, that was about bringing in the back office. HR, billing, accounting, customer service—they could all be brought back into the fold at Bayless. Administratively, I knew we could become very strong.

I also knew that if we had the best administration, technology, and infrastructure, we could attract the best clinical professionals to our practice. At the turn of the year, these changes bore fruit. Angie Renshaw was a CPA and had joined me and the company as our controller. She helped me establish a firm financial accounting and back-office system that would prepare us for our growth to come. In January, I hired Dr. Andrea Raby to be our chief psychiatrist, filling an extremely important position at the company. We'd long wanted to branch out beyond behavioral care with our treatment options, but to do that, we needed someone like Dr. Raby on staff. Now, we had her. As a bonus, Dr. Raby joined the team as a true believer in our mission, bringing in raw passion for improving patient care.

In February 2015, I found a new pediatrician in Dr. Robert James. Like me, Dr. James was a Morehouse man, and I convinced him of my vision. It was a watershed moment for Bayless. After he signed on, other doctors and caregivers began to see us as a credible facility and a good place to work. We filled our roster in short order.

Before long, I would also meet Dr. Katie Brite at a meeting. She became the chief of our primary care team. Dr. Brite was the type of brilliant physician administrator we'd been sorely lacking.

Bringing in this new level of leadership offered a lot of advantage to the company, but it also represented a challenge. I'd always been the person to take the lead on everything. Dad had taught me to spend part of each day walking around and talking to the team. But as the company was growing bigger, I had to learn how to hand leadership, responsibility, and that in-person contact off to people like Dr. Raby, Dr. James, and Dr. Brite.

I also had to find ways to build relationships with people who were often older, better educated, and more experienced than me—some of whom came from very different backgrounds. I was a young Black man who was asking all of these people to trust me with their careers and livelihoods.

Dad had always taught me to seek out commonality with everyone, to find the type of connection that could allow us to grab a beer after work and have a productive, enjoyable conversation. I found now that I also needed to prove to my team that they were right to trust me. And to do that, I felt I had to put some quick wins up on the board that would show there was good reason to follow me as I took some massive swings.

The quick win I focused on was taking on more adult patients and focusing on drug treatment aimed at addressing the opioid crisis. By spring, these changes helped us finally see some profitability. Acknowledging that I'd steered the ship through the storm, so to speak, Dad pulled me aside one day and asked me to refocus on telehealth.

"You figured out this integration thing. Now figure out telehealth!"

Compared with our last push for telemedicine, things were looking much more promising. This was, after all, a new era in technology. As Dad reminded me, everyone now had an iPhone, internet connections were much faster, and technology costs were down. If we could make telehealth operationally effective for the clinicians, our patients might now be ready and able to give it a try. This could be our moment.

It was a compelling argument, and I agreed. In April, I began looking for solutions that would help us facilitate "mobile health," as we called it at the time, testing different companies to determine which ones could work hand in hand with the systems we already had in place.

Things in my personal life were also trending up. I'd proposed to Jamil in June 2014, surprising her on a trip to Puerto Vallarta ten months into our relationship. A year on, our wedding was now fast approaching.

Meanwhile, we began to see concrete changes occurring with integrated care on the state level. We had continued to fight the Medicaid payers for children's services, and Arizona was finally paying attention. The director of AHCCCS spent a day with me at the clinic, observing our revolutionary operational flow and integrated system. Shortly after, he asked me to present our concept and business model to his team. This was potentially the opportunity we'd been looking for to change some minds and change the whole system.

Before I could focus on any of that, though, I had to focus on getting married. And I had to deliver some bad news. Dad wanted to go to my bachelor's party, but I turned him down. He was understandably upset. He was still very close with Kyle and many of my other friends. But I thought he'd feel awkward on the night out. Besides, it was on his birthday—June 7. A few days later, he called me to go to dinner to celebrate belatedly, but I turned him down again. It wasn't malicious. I was simply overwhelmed. While the business was running a bit more smoothly, there was still so much to do. And then there were wedding preparations to consider. Jamil's car had also broken down, so we were sharing one ride. There just wasn't time.

Or so I felt at that moment. Turning down that dinner is one of the greatest regrets of my life.

"Son, everything's going to be okay," he told me on that call. "We'll talk again real soon."

I've often wondered if Dad had a sense this might be our last conversation. He was a very intelligent man, and I have to think he knew he was growing weaker. We'd had our share of arguments in the previous few months, and he had been so gentle on that call, almost as if it were a goodbye.

The next morning, I was on the freeway, driving out of Phoenix to meet a telemedicine vendor. Dad was playing golf with Frank Johnson. I wasn't too far from the course where they were teeing off.

Then, I got the call from my mom. Frank had called her hysterical. Dad had dropped over on the golf course.

I turned around and raced to him. By the time I got there, though, he was gone.

A Scramble to Save Everything

I was ready to quit. Although we'd seen some gains, the company was still in serious trouble, especially after the Rainbow debacle. And I was distraught. Losing Dad was bigger than losing the most important man in my life—I'd just lost my business partner and someone who had always believed in me. After I'd convinced him of my vision, he was 100 percent in my corner, no matter what setbacks I'd experienced. He was my greatest mentor; he was my best friend. It seemed incredibly unfair that I'd come through my health scare only to lose my dad.

It was so difficult, I had to be medicated for several days. The pain and the despair I was feeling were literally too much for me to bear.

It didn't help that I couldn't step away from the business. On July 1, just three short weeks after Dad's death and a little over a month before my wedding, I got a letter from our bank stating their intent to foreclose on the business. Dad was the sole guarantor on the very first commercial mortgage loan, and without him, all of Bayless was at risk. Once again, I had to scramble.

Mom came to the rescue and connected me to someone she knew at Comerica bank. It saved the business, but it also meant I—and I alone—was now on the line for everything. Looking back, I can see how the experience taught me a lot about my pain threshold as an entrepreneur. I could have gone to investors, sold equity, and alleviated a lot of the discomfort I experienced during that time—but I knew bootstrapping debt would prove to be much cheaper than losing equity. It was the right call. Even so, putting my assets on the line brought another level of stress.

For the first time in my life, I felt I needed professional emotional support. Before that brutal summer, I'd spent years running a mental health company but never done counseling myself. This seemed like a good time to start. I hired a therapist to do sessions in my office. Everyone at Bayless assumed he was a contractor, and I didn't correct them.

That may strike you as strange—after all, my office was the last place someone should need to hide the support they needed for their mental health. But I'd grown up in a community that still looked distrustfully at therapy. And though I didn't share those feelings myself, some part of me was uncomfortable showing my team just how much I was struggling. I'd always been strong—relentless—no matter what I was facing. I was a leader, and I felt I had to keep putting on that courageous face for everyone at Bayless, even if those who knew me knew it was a front.

In the moment, I could almost laugh at the irony. It turned out I might have been a very good candidate for telehealth. Dad was really onto something there.

A Wedding, a Funeral, a Blessing

Jamil and I had spent the past year looking forward to our wedding. Yet, I almost asked her to put it off.

My father's funeral in June felt like all the ceremony I could handle for a while. It was a massive event that showed me just how many lives he'd touched. Hundreds of people showed up, and each one of them loved Dad. Each one of them admired him for all he stood for.

Bayless/Tubbs Family Dinner after Dad's Passing

I wish I could have dwelt on that positive moment and taken some solace, but it wasn't possible for me to slow down. Unfortunately, on top of everything else, I discovered Dad hadn't had his will in order. That meant we also had to go through probate to sort out his estate. With banks and court, the company still on the ropes, and the strain of fighting the whole Arizona medical system, I didn't know if I could also take on a wedding.

Jamil was incredibly understanding, even pushing me to cancel. She approached me on multiple occasions and told me it was fine to postpone. I was in such obvious pain, she wanted to give me time to grieve.

"I'll wait as long as necessary," she told me. "I'm not going anywhere."

I nearly agreed. I wrestled with the possibility for a long time. In the end, I decided that having the wedding now was the right call.

Our wedding took place on August 8, in Woodland, Washington, about an hour north of Portland. True to the typical Pacific Northwest climate, it was cloudy and gray all day. The weather seemed to fit the ceremony. Acting as a family reunion as much as a wedding, the event was incredibly emotional for me and everyone else. The somber and the joyful mixed together uneasily throughout the afternoon.

But it ended well. The day was capped perfectly with a family photo. Just as everyone gathered together, the sun burst through the clouds and a double rainbow appeared overhead.

Jamil and Justin Wedding Photo

As we all gathered around the camera to take a look at the image, Aunt Ila spoke what everyone else seemed to be thinking: "Your dad never would miss an opportunity for a photo."

We all broke down in tears—because we knew how right she was. Dad was there in spirit. He was always the center of attention in every room he entered, and now he was showing up at my wedding to claim the spotlight—like he always had. I wouldn't have had it any other way. I'd never been happier to be in his shadow.

That rainbow coming through the clouds represented the first real moment of healing. It also represented a change in the weather for Bayless. Shortly after the wedding, Arizona announced it was finally switching to an integrated health model for Medicaid. After years of struggle and loss, the light was breaking through, and we could finally see a way forward. Bayless Integrated Healthcare was now leading the charge for a new care delivery system.

7

A NEW JURNI

I was overjoyed by my marriage, but the months-long stretch between the Rainbow Pediatrics ordeal and settling my dad's probate had exhausted my already depleted mental and physical resources. Between filing a lawsuit against the pediatrician who walked out, losing my dad, opening the probate, planning a wedding, finishing the probate, moving banking relationships, and tying the knot, my capacity for peripheral concerns was rapidly diminishing.

Adding to the pressure I was under, the director of AHCCCS called an all-provider and health plan leadership meeting at a conference center in Tempe, Arizona. He asked me to join a panel onstage to discuss how Arizona could move forward with integrated health and to outline potential problems and solutions—in front of the very people who'd been fighting me over the new delivery system.

When the panel began, I started presenting as planned. Everything went well, until one of my provider competitors interrupted my presentation to accuse me of trying to turn Arizona's public healthcare into a privatized system. While he had the audience's attention, he ravaged the idea, insisting it was "not how public health works."

People in the room began to laugh. It wasn't the first time I'd experienced that reaction on my journey, but this time it really rattled me. I left the event pissed off and even more motivated to prove everyone wrong.

The one positive thing I noticed during the presentation was that the director never laughed.

In fact, it seemed several points I made about integrated care made perfect sense to the director of AHCCCS. After the *Arizona Republic* profile of the RBHA system, he seemed determined to shake things up. And in December 2015, he made his move. That month, the director announced that Arizona would be making the largest Medicaid transition in American history. The state would be moving to an integrated care model. The rollout would be included in a six-year contract and required a $54 billion investment to redefine how healthcare would be delivered. A date was set to begin the transition: October 1, 2018.

It was an incredible triumph. I only wish Dad had been with me to celebrate. But it also meant I had a lot more to do to make sure Bayless Integrated Healthcare could take full advantage in a few years. I couldn't afford extra distractions anymore. So at the end of 2015, when I learned that we'd gotten our shares of the company back from the bankruptcy proceedings against the former Rainbow doctor, I decided to drop the lawsuit against him. I didn't have the energy to pursue it. And besides, I found it far more motivating to make sure he regretted his choice to leave Bayless. The old chip was back on the shoulder where it belonged.

Besides, I had bigger issues to deal with. With the changes at AHCCCS, I had new ambitious plans for Bayless, and I needed to bring my team together. And soon, I'd also have to focus far more attention on my family.

Building a New Community

In January 2016, Bayless embarked on a new initiative: our diamond strategy. With the state finally shifting to an integrated care model, I wanted to maximize our impact across Phoenix. To do this, we launched an effort to open four new locations on each compass point around the city to provide care to everyone—creating a diamond formation around Phoenix. Those clinics, combined with the central locations we already had, would allow us to serve the entire city. We also opened a second administration center.

Success in this effort was going to require immense buy-in from the team. The Rainbow acquisition, the failure to become an FQHC, and other major initiatives had caused so many big disruptions over the last few years, and I couldn't deny at this point that my leadership had done some damage while I dragged the company forward. People were still suspicious of telehealth, and the team had never been completely on board with my vision.

It was time to change that. I needed to focus on becoming a better leader. For Dad, this had been seemingly effortless. He could naturally make an ally out of anyone—from the Goldwater family to skeptical doctors and psychiatrists. Now that he was gone, repairing relationships with my team was all the more important.

This would require growth on my part, but it would also take more clarity on what we were trying to do. Inspired by books of Jim Collins—particularly *Good to Great* and *Built to Last*—I realized that for too long, the vision for the company had been too complicated. Collins introduced me to the "hedgehog concept" that would help simplify where we were trying to go. It required me to answer three basic questions about the business: What was I passionate about? What drove our economic engine? And what could we be the best in the world at?

I meditated upon these questions until clarity came to me. It took me back to basics. I realized what I was most passionate about—what really drove me—was the fact that so many people needed mental healthcare urgently and couldn't get it. I thought back to the FQHC I visited and all the people who would probably never see a mental health professional because it took too long and was just too difficult. If we could change that, we could be the best in the world at getting people the care they needed on the timeline they needed it. And that would drive our business forward.

At that point, it all clicked into place. I returned to my initial inspiration behind integrated care. As I had realized back then, Bayless should give people in need of mental health assistance access to a licensed professional within seventy-two hours of the request.

That was it. That was the vision. That vision would allow us to track our progress and to flag whenever we failed. It would also give us a clear strategy to increase our volume of patients and to scale.

A simplified, clearer vision would help bring the team together, but there was still a lot to do on my end. I had to become the right leader for this organization.

Before I took on that challenge, though, I needed to recharge. Luckily, that's when Craig called. Craig and Esther had just pseudo-retired. They hired a new CEO to run the day-to-day for their company, and they purchased property in the Spanish countryside. Their plan was to live half the year in Spain for the rest of their lives, and they wanted Jamil and I to share part of their first summer in their new condo in Pamplona. Jamil and I eagerly agreed to the plan.

It was only two weeks, but that trip was one of the best of my life. Craig took me around the wine region and really developed my palate. I had never had the opportunity to get to know wine before that, but Craig's experience creating high-end, luxury wine baskets left him with an incredible knowledge of the region and its wineries. We visited a few of them. For the first time, I really understood and enjoyed wine.

Justin, Jamil, Esther, Craig and Debbie

We did the running of the bulls, and Esther—who had a master's in art—toured us around Barcelona, giving us all kinds of facts and history about Spanish art. It was an incredible experience. After all the years of struggle, stress, and loss, it was exactly what I needed.

The only downside was that Esther began feeling fatigued and thought she had a cold coming on. We wouldn't know for some time how much more serious her condition was. Later, we would discover she was at the start of a long battle that would end in all of us losing her. But that was still years in the future, and her unexplained tiredness was the only cloud on an otherwise sunny Spanish dream vacation.

In addition to mentoring me through the wine regions of Spain, Craig was still actively mentoring my business endeavors.

I really needed that mentorship, because I was soon to discover the need to cut ties with several members of my CEO peer group.

I had joined a CEO peer organization in 2014. The group had been instrumental in helping me recognize my need to develop further as a leader. The members urged me to look inside myself and find solutions to the problems that kept popping up. They helped me learn how to adjust while remaining authentic to who I was. Along with my leadership development coaches, they gave me the guidance and support to develop the new skill sets and tools that I was planning to implement as I aimed to connect with my team without losing myself in the process.

I still had a ways to go to grow into a leader who could inspire a whole team—a leader who could speak to people with different learning styles and life experiences. My peer group was helping me bridge that gap.

But in 2016, suddenly, there were problems with that peer group. Our group included one Asian woman and one Hispanic man, but I was the only Black person. I was also the youngest member, and I had the smallest company. But that didn't particularly bother me. There was always a lot to learn from CEOs who were much older and very different from me. One of the other members even became a billionaire while I was part of the group.

I respected the other members and considered them my mentors and friends. But in the spring of 2016, at a meeting I hosted at an area country club, I began to notice that things seemed a little . . . different.

The meeting began normally enough. I set up my PowerPoint—it was my turn to introduce my company to the group—and then excused myself to use the restroom. When I came back, my presentation was no longer up on the display. Instead, someone was playing a video making fun of Hillary Clinton. Everyone was laughing like it was the funniest thing they'd ever seen. I thought it was a little strange, but I didn't say anything.

I am not a particularly strident political person. Living in Arizona, you meet people of all political stripes, and you can make friends and do business with everyone. Dad, after all, was a good friend of Bob Goldwater. But as we all know, we were entering different times, and I was soon to see an uglier side of many of my friends.

After the chair of the CEO group reassured me that this was a one-time slip, he took a private poll of everyone present. It turned out all but four of the sixteen members were voting for Donald Trump.

I was shocked. I started asking questions about why people were willing to excuse his behavior and was met with responses that danced around the topic by turning to taxes and policy. This behavior, and my discomfort, continued throughout the election season. At another meeting that summer, the group brought in a national security leader under President Reagan who spent the entire session bashing Obama's policies. No one was invited to counter that argument. The atmosphere in our meetings had clearly shifted.

Things came to a head the morning after the election. I attended a meeting at a conservative northern Scottsdale home. That morning, I woke up to Jamil in tears. She was struggling with the shock and uncertainty of what was ahead. All the way to the meeting, my phone was blowing up with people in my community who were distraught over the election results. Some people we treated were worried their family would be deported. Others were so concerned by the turn of events that they couldn't get out of bed and go to work. I even got a call from my COO informing me that a patient in our lobby was bloodied from a fight he'd gotten in outside our front doors.

I felt an immense amount of empathy for my community, and the weight of that empathy was almost overwhelming. I was still trying to hold it together when I drove up to the Vistage meeting, where I discovered everyone out on the lawn drinking champagne.

I got out of my car, and one of them called out to me.

"We didn't even think you would show up, Justin."

I lost my shit.

"This is a disgrace," I said. "You have no idea what other people in the world are going through. I have family, patients, and employees who are really struggling with this, and you're mocking me?"

The chair took me aside and tried to calm me. He said the group needed to talk about it.

"I don't even know why you're so upset," one of the CEOs scoffed. "My son and all his friends are all celebrating too."

I asked whether his son had grown up in that conservative northern Scottsdale neighborhood and what his exposure to other populations had been. Sure enough, he'd been born right there in the center of privilege. He'd grown up in a big house, attended a private school in the same community, and shared that region's singular worldview with all his similarly affluent friends. I reminded him that not all young people had that viewpoint. Not every young person was excited about the future with Trump as president.

Saying that calmed me somewhat, but the last straw came at lunch—when one of the CEOs told me that the whole situation, from Trump's behavior to the election results, was Obama's fault because he treated Muslims better than Christians. Then the chair, who'd positioned himself as the peacemaker of the group, came over and repeated the same thing.

Once again, I was floored. I had grown close with this group—they knew personal things about my dad, my family, and my business. They knew the struggles we'd faced as individuals who weren't born into the same privilege as others.

I stood up, told them that this was my last meeting, and walked out.

I wish I could say this sort of reaction was limited to that group. But that year I found out many of my close friends shared those feelings. Crucially, these were not just people who had conservative views or liked Republican economic policy. They bought into that cult-like attitude around Trump and the rhetoric that targeted underrepresented people.

That year was a transformative one for our nation and for me personally. I had to take a hard look at my relationships, and I needed to find new sources of support.

Luckily, I had other places to turn. I'd played in a golf tournament over the summer and met police Lieutenant Timothy Woods. I learned that he was the vice polemarch of the Western region of Kappa Alpha Psi—my dad's old fraternity, of which he'd been a charter member. We struck up a conversation about my dad and golf, and Tim recommended I connect with the fraternity.

I'd always wanted to be part of Kappa, but the Morehouse chapter wasn't active during my time there because of some extracurricular behavior. I was deeply motivated to join not only because it was my dad's old fraternity, but because of the opportunity to enjoy Tim's mentorship while so many of my relationships were in flux.

As soon as I was initiated, I made a point of helping those who would come after me. I didn't believe in being part of a community solely for my benefit. That wasn't how I ran Bayless, and it wasn't how I'd behave as a brother of Kappa Alpha Psi. With that intention in mind, I created a scholarship fund to help young men in high school who want to pursue health sciences. I also started a golf tournament in Dad's name.

Lifting Hooves

Slowly getting my footing back, I turned back to my aim to improve my leadership. In the midst of the election and the turmoil at my CEO peer group, Bayless had managed to open our first new location as part of the diamond strategy. Bayless Therapeutic Wellness opened in central Phoenix in October 2016.

We'd also won our first Health Choice Center of Excellence award, which is given to providers providing exceptional care and services. The award is designed to highlight providers with high levels of patient satisfaction, leadership, and innovation, among other qualities.

Center of Excellence Award by Health Choice Arizona

As we pushed forward on the next location, I reviewed key cultural points in our company, and I quickly realized that our annual retreats in Phoenix didn't do enough to strengthen our team. We needed to put more distance between ourselves and our obligations to really be able to focus on the organization. Beginning in 2017, then, we would take our annual retreat elsewhere. That way we could focus on the future and what we could do as a team.

For our first retreat, I relied on Dad's judgment. In 2011, I'd gone down to Tucson with him and the team to help convince them of the value of integrated care. There, we visited a horse whisperer and therapist named Wyatt Webb. Wyatt is very well known in celebrity circles, having been recommended by Oprah, among others.

It was a lot of fun, and I thought the team would enjoy going back. For many, it would be their first visit.

At the beginning of our session, Wyatt instructed us to approach his horse one at a time and raise its hoof. None of our confident and assured doctors could do it. As each person tried and failed, Wyatt asked them questions and provided commentary on their approaches. By the end of the exercise, half of them were crying and the other half were pissed. He basically broke them all down.

I was the last to make the attempt. Approaching the horse, I assumed Wyatt wouldn't remember me. But to my great surprise, Wyatt knew exactly who I was. Determined to make the right impression on the team, I managed to lift the hoof.

But if I thought that meant I'd get off easy, I was wrong.

"You lifted it forcefully," Wyatt observed. "Could you have lifted it a different way?"

Wyatt continued challenging me. He painted a much bigger purpose for Bayless Integrated Healthcare than I could see at that point. And then he brought it back to Dad. Before long, he was talking to me about transitions, about building a family and a unit that everyone believed in. He kept coming back to some advice my father had given me about taking care of others and passing something on. He used the entire session to focus on the future through knowing what would be best for our families and kids.

It tore me up. I realized that the relentless mentality I'd prided myself on was a double-edged sword. Yes, I accomplished things. But for the first time, I truly began to realize that those accomplishments came at a steep cost. Had I been too forceful moving toward integrated care? Could I have brought people along better? Had I been too headstrong in purchasing Rainbow Pediatrics? Could I have made better choices if I'd been a little less determined?

I thought back to my first six months at Bayless, how I'd sat in my office during the Christmas party, trying to fix everything instead of getting to know the team. I thought of my initial instinct to install the EOS system on my own instead of bringing in an expert and trusting them to get it right. Far too often, I'd tried to do it all alone and simply expected others to follow. For years, I used brute force and pressure to make things happen.

Force had allowed me to change the company, but it had also led to the hurt feelings and suspicion within the company I was now trying to repair. Going forward, I'd need to work on how I lifted any future hooves—and maybe find a way for the team to lift those hooves together.

That gave me a lot to ponder. On the trip back, I mostly stayed out of the conversation. Anyway, everyone was talking about getting back to their kids, and I didn't have any—yet.

That was about to change. When I got home, Jamil was in the kitchen. I flopped onto the couch and closed my eyes. She came over to me.

"Hey, look up," she said. "I'm pregnant."

Unexpected Blessing

It was surreal. Wyatt had just been speaking about transitions and my dad's passing, and suddenly I was about to become a father.

Jamil's news left me with an indelible impression: I was 100 percent certain I was having a son. The first born of every Bayless I knew of, going as far back as I could trace, was a boy. The symmetry in my own life was too compelling to ignore. I'd lost my dad. Now, I was certain I would have a son so that I could build the same sort of relationship with him as I'd had with my father.

When I found out the baby was a girl, I was more than taken aback; I didn't know what to do. I was a leader, someone used to taking charge, but I didn't know how to raise a girl. I'd grown up in a male-dominated, testosterone-heavy household. Even my mom was a tomboy. I had no idea what to expect or what to do. I was completely flummoxed.

Until I saw her face. Then, everything clicked.

Jurni was born on 9/11. The significance of the date did not escape me. In the first place, fatherhood was definitely a 9-1-1 emergency. But Jurni's birthday also had echoes of the day Dad passed—9/11, 6/11. It was Dad communicating all over again.

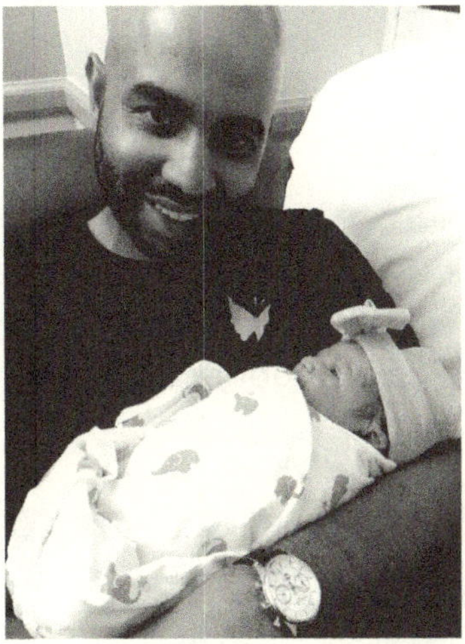

Justin and Jurni

And that communication was about more than just dates. When Jurni proved to be a real hellion in her first few months, Jamil and I assumed it was because we didn't know how to "do" parenting yet. But Jurni's forceful personality has stayed with her. What I realized was that despite not having a son, I had the spirit of my father back. Jurni was loud, boisterous, and rebellious, just like Dad. She has the same jovial nature, the same playfulness, the same shrewdness—just in a female form. Six to nine: she flipped the script, but the same spirit was there. It wouldn't be the relationship I expected, but it was the one I needed.

Having Jurni really changed my perspective on what was important in life. With her around, I gradually started to realize that all the strain and stress I endured and generated while trying to create a better life needed to change. Dad had been focused on the same thing—providing a better life for his sons—and as a result, he wasn't there for a lot of the big moments in my childhood. With that realization, a seed was planted: I could do things a little differently. I could be a bigger part of my kids' lives.

Eventually, that thought would manifest in big changes for the Bayless clan and the Bayless business.

Work and Life

While I was waiting to meet Jurni, I'd kept myself busy. In May of that year, I consolidated the Rainbow locations into a new integrated health center. I opened it on May 1, the thirty-fifth anniversary of the date my dad founded the company. I dedicated the center to him.

Justin dedicating the opening of the
Bayless Integrated Health Center to his Father

I'd also opened the next location in our diamond strategy: Dobson Ranch, which covered the east side of the city. I got to do that one with three generations of the most important women in my life: Mom, Jamil, and Jurni just about ready to come and join us.

Mom, Justin and Jamil at Bayless Integrated Healthcare
Dobson Ranch Opening

That same month, I won the Health Care Hero Award.

After Jurni was born, things didn't slow down at work. Two months after receiving the Hero Award, I was given the ASU Spirit of Enterprise Award.

In March the following year, I launched my podcast, *Relentless Mentality*.

At this point, I was managing a large network of integrated care facilities, a large team, and a podcast. I was also making continual efforts to add telehealth capabilities to the business and preparing us for the Medicaid transition to integrated care. And I was trying to be an active and present father. Things were going well, but I was spinning a lot of plates.

To keep myself motivated, I had an Inky Johnson quote on my desk: "If you keep going, you won't regret it. If you give up, you will."

This period of good fortune reached its zenith in October 2018. On October 1, Arizona officially switched over to an integrated healthcare system.

That same month, we opened the west-side addition to our diamond clinic strategy: Avondale. This one was particularly important because it was the first location designed to treat an entire school district.

That would have been enough for any month, but October was also the month the University of Arizona retired Jerryd's jersey.

Jerryd, Mom, and Justin at Jerryd's induction to University of Arizona Basketball Jersey Retirement

The Bayless family wasn't done with that October yet. That very month, Jamil graduated with her degree as a nurse practitioner. It was the end of a long, incredibly challenging road for her. She'd gone back to school in the fall of 2016, and nothing had been able to knock her off course. Four days after she had Jurni, she was back on campus doing rotations. She knew if she took a break, she might never get the chance to finish. Somehow, she found a way to take on pregnancy, motherhood, and grad school all at once and come out on top.

And she wasn't done yet. At her graduation, we announced she was pregnant again. Nothing was going to stop her from building her career and her family.

A few months later, in January 2019, we learned that Jamil was pregnant with twins. Jamil wasn't surprised at all. She'd had a sense since she was about eleven that she'd have twins. It had been one of the first questions she'd asked the doctor when she first became pregnant with Jurni. Now, her prophecy was proving accurate.

I was less prepared for twins, but I was confident of one thing: I was finally going to have a son. The odds seemed pretty decent this time. There wasn't any good reason for my focus on having a son. Perhaps it was some misogynistic assumption about the value of sons—something tracing back to the need for an heir. Regardless, I grew so confident, I actually began to think a son was a guarantee. Without any evidence, I started telling everyone the babies were twin boys.

I was wrong again.

At a follow-up appointment, Jamil and I learned they were, in fact, identical little girls: Justice and Joy. When I heard the news, I froze. I might have even fainted for a moment. When I came to myself, we were back in the car.

I hadn't said a word since I found out. I was just in shock. Jamil kept comforting me and telling me everything was going to be fine. I'm sure she secretly thought my reaction was funny, but she was good enough not to show it. Other members of my family showed less restraint when they heard about it. The story made my mom's entire year. Now, even I can see the humor. But in the moment, I'd just experienced a major blow.

I started the car but didn't put it in drive yet. The radio came on. We were listening to SiriusXM, and the name of a song scrolled across as it began to play.

Suddenly, we lost signal. Without changing the title of the song, a different one blared out. It was the very beginning of Stevie Wonder's "Isn't She Lovely." For about five seconds, the car was filled with the sound of Stevie's baby daughter crying. Then, the most joyful music kicked in.

Jamil and I knew instantly it was another message from Dad. He was telling me that this was going to be an adventure—for me *and* my four lovely women.

As Stevie started crooning, Jamil and I both started crying.

8

BETTER TOGETHER

For years, the main focus at Bayless had been on integrated health, but we'd never stopped trying to do telehealth. Despite the setbacks we had when we first tried to pilot a program, and the disruption after Dad passed, we'd continued testing out models, software, and hardware options as they came to market. We tried to develop a program for our psychology department. Nothing ever quite worked, but I felt we were getting closer.

The chief medical officer of AHCCCS took an interest in our efforts back in 2016. She supported our tests and pilots and asked to be kept informed about our progress.

It was great receiving encouragement from the top of AHCCCS. Still, we couldn't find the breakthrough we'd had with integrated care—until 2018.

It helped that we were well ahead of the competition with integrated care. We had already opened our flagship integrated health clinic, and we were proving out the vision I'd developed a decade before.

That gave us the space to focus on fulfilling Dad's vision of telehealth. And it created the potential to integrate it into our integrated care system. If I could merge both systems, we'd have a meeting of the two core visions at the heart of the company.

Just over the horizon, I could see an apotheosis of my time at Bayless. Dad brought me in to push telehealth, a dream he'd had for decades. As soon as I took over, I pushed for integrated care. Over time, my vision took precedence. But now that we'd won that battle, we were finally on the cusp of merging our ideas and achieving both.

If only Dad were there to enjoy the moment with me.

A New Reality

The transition to an integrated health model brought another win to mental health patients in the state of Arizona: the block grants I'd been fighting for so long were finally gone. We no longer had to hit a particular dollar amount or limit the care we provided to hit a target. Patient funding was now a free market system, and we could now truly treat our community.

Because some patients require much more diagnostics and care than others, we had always wanted our highest-level clinicians to assess each patient and create an individualized care plan at the very beginning of their treatment. The block grant system had limited our ability to do that. It forced us to ration care so we could ensure our funding provided for our entire patient base. In the process, it put patients whose needs exceeded the baseline of care at a major disadvantage.

The new fee-for-service model took away the need for such rationing. If we needed to provide additional services for a patient, we could do that without worrying about funding. Funding now followed patient needs instead of a nonsensical system that limited care.

It was a huge win. The change empowered patients to choose providers who gave the best care—and, for the first time, it incentivized those providers to prioritize better services and quality care over worrying they might run out of funds. Since we'd always been focused on comprehensive, individualized care at Bayless, we were leading the care model in the new free-market system. The days of corruption enabled by the block grant system had ended, and I couldn't have been happier.

As technology continued to get faster and cheaper, telemedicine was also more realistic than ever. If anything, technology could now save us money. We could now move many services online and avoid any more expensive, new brick-and-mortar growth. Doing things in the virtual space would decrease our overhead, even as we continued to grow. The question was no longer one of possibility. Instead, we turned our focus to figuring out the best way for telemedicine to fit the interconnected ecosystem we'd created.

But to make this big leap into telehealth, I'd need buy-in from my whole team. And that meant I needed to make good on my efforts to be a better leader. I wasn't going to force the horse's hoof up this time. I was going to find a better way to convince my people.

Chi-Town

I had been championing telemedicine for years, but the entire leadership team was still against it. Many were still scarred from our first attempt when it was too expensive. Even as I tried to convince them on a financial level, leadership now brought up the risk of malpractice suits and the difficulty of providing a level of care equal to what we could deliver in person. Another huge roadblock to telehealth was the limited options for formal training. Even today, physicians have a plethora of opportunities for continuing education, but telehealth isn't typically one of them.

The fact that I wasn't a physician or clinician made it difficult to argue that we could provide consistent, excellent care within a technological ecosystem. Approaching the discussion from a business perspective, I provided research reports that showed telemedicine could be an even more effective modality of care for certain populations and certain conditions. But my team still held hard-won reservations that came from years of education and practice.

Fitting the trend in my life, most of our clinical leadership were women—women who were older, more experienced, and more knowledgeable than me. In that room, I was yet again the only brother. And I was conscious that it was a bad look to try to lecture them into accepting my view on the matter. Although I wholeheartedly believed in telehealth, I knew I'd have to find a way to prove to them that this was the right way forward.

I settled on the American Telemedicine Association conference in Chicago. At an annual planning session in January 2018, I announced it—and I'm not ashamed to say I bribed everyone to join me.

Doctors are required to earn a certain number of Continuing Medical Education credits (CMEs) to maintain their license. I used that to my advantage. I told them I'd cover all their expenses if they came with me to the conference. Even if they came away as skeptical of telehealth as they were at the moment, they'd get a free trip, a stay at a very nice hotel, and the chance to earn a few more CMEs. There was no downside!

My goal was to get enough buy-in to get everyone to test telehealth across all our service lines. I knew that once I got everyone to Chicago, I could do what I do best: explain the vision to each of them one by one while also wining and dining the whole group in Chi-town. I planned to spend a day covering telehealth through the lens of each specialization with a member of leadership, one day on mental health, one on psychiatry, and one on primary care. The final day would be spent with the whole group, focused specifically on technology and how it could make our system better. I hoped the tour would be enough to get a wholehearted commitment from each member of the team.

Everyone was excited for the trip, but Dr. Raby and Dr. Brite, in particular, were far less enthusiastic about the telehealth focus. Dr. Raby told me that she had always believed in my integrated care mission, but she was suspicious whether telehealth appointments could replicate the quality of an inpatient visit.

The conference was held at the McCormick Center—a behemoth with 2.5 million square feet of event space. This was a major upgrade on the last telehealth event I'd been to a decade ago that didn't even fill a small ballroom and had only reserved a few hundred square feet for technology. This time, there were two football fields' worth of technology—a sign that the technological component of telehealth had truly arrived. The massive cameras and TVs we'd seen strapped to carts in 2009 had been replaced with sleek wearables, smartphones, software, and everything in between.

Bayless Integrated Healthcare Clinical Leadership and Justin in Chicago at the American Telemedicine Association Conference

The tech displays really drove home a point to the team. Despite all the advances, the Bayless leadership still thought they needed "peripherals"—additional technological devices that would allow a doctor to check vitals—and a physical visit to diagnose patients with certain conditions properly and accurately. But the conference made a strong case that this was no longer true. We now had the Apple Watch that tracked vitals. We also had virtual waiting room apps that could transfer patients in an organized way, as if they were in the real office. In short, we had more technological options that enabled doctors and clinicians to make most assessments over the call and see patients in a systematic, effective way.

I had long envisioned a world that was front door virtual—one in which we only brought people into the clinic when it was necessary—and the technology was finally on the market to make that a reality. If a patient did need to have an assessment or test that could only be done in person, our diamond strategy across the Valley ensured a location was always close enough to be convenient.

The conference also addressed the team's other concerns. Leaders in telemedicine from both the US and Canada explained how the current laws in both countries made the modality possible, and they explained how they'd integrated it into their own practices. We also met with several governing bodies. The American Psychiatric Association and the American Academy of Family Physicians each gave four-hour seminars, and Dr. Raby, Dr Brite, and I attended them both.

Finally, we got a glimpse into the future of counseling: how technology could allow people to enter a virtual clinic through an avatar environment and get anonymous care.

By the last day, I'd begun to notice an undercurrent of excitement in my team, but I made sure not to push too hard to get their impressions. I kept the horse whisperer's advice in mind and made sure not to press my advantage. I let the impressions sink in and let them make their own determinations.

I vividly remember the end of the final day. I settled into the front seat of our Uber SUV and noticed an unusual quiet from my team as we made our way to the airport. When I turned around to see what was going on, they were all writing in notebooks.

"What are you doing?" I asked.

"Strategizing," came the reply. "On how we're going to implement telemedicine company wide as soon as we get back."

I turned back around with a smile on my face. I'd secured my buy-in.

My team had locked into what Dad and I had been saying for years. They'd seen that telemedicine was an opportunity for Bayless to be ahead of the curve again. They'd also seen that it could create a better quality of life for our providers by eliminating hours of transportation and relieving them of the monotony of sitting in an office all day. They could work from home and structure their lives in a way that was better suited to their needs. Most importantly, it would remove barriers for patients. They, too, would save that transportation time. As Dad had always envisioned, they'd be more likely to pursue care if they could do it from their phone while in the car or sitting in their own living room. And they wouldn't face the anxiety around visiting a physical location and worrying they'd be judged their peers.

When I got back to Phoenix, the chief medical advisor at Bayless, Dr. Pelberg, said, "I don't know what you did, but you've won them over. They're convinced this is the future."

I could honestly say I hadn't done anything. "They saw for themselves that the technology and timing are right. Now it's up to us to help them put it all together."

Although he'd never been a true believer before, he agreed. From that moment on, things began to flow naturally. I didn't need to push anymore.

More than that, I learned an important leadership lesson: while this was still my vision—and my father's—it was no longer my burden to carry alone. The entire team fully embraced and supported it.

Ready for a New Era

By 2019, we were finally in a position to really move on telehealth. The team was on board, our flagship office at South Mountain had reopened—thus checking off the south side of our diamond strategy—and AHCCCS decided it wanted our opinion on how telemedicine could change protocols to improve patient access to mental healthcare. We'd been on the frontlines of developing telehealth options in Arizona for a long time by that point, and it put us in a unique position to identify potential problems, fixes, and opportunities to deliver the most value to the state. It didn't hurt that in 2018 Bayless had made the Inc. 5000 list, which marked us out as one of the fastest-growing private companies in the country. We'd stay on that list for as long as I was running the company. Around the same time, I'd been named on the "40 under 40" list by the *Phoenix Business Journal*.

In my ongoing conversations with the CMO at AHCCCS, I identified things from billing, coding, and location perspectives that could be improved. The CMO continued to be an enthusiastic ally in this effort and shepherded in the changes.

On October 1, 2019—the one-year anniversary of our triumph for integrated care—the state shifted priorities to make Arizona a leader in telemedicine. It also changed outdated guidelines to pave the way forward. Before, guidelines dependent on the major payers (Medicaid, Medicare, and commercial) dictated where clinicians and patients could be located while providing and receiving telemedical care. Essentially, they required patients to be physically present in a licensed clinical location, even if they were on a screen. The rules also varied depending on the service being provided. Mental health and primary care had different requirements and limitations. It was all unnecessarily complicated.

Now, we finally had those issues resolved. After October, patients could receive care anywhere—at their home, in their car, at the park—on their personal mobile device. From that point on, we had a green light to implement telemedicine across our entire organization.

That same month, we opened the last of our diamond facilities, covering the north side of the Phoenix metro area with our location at Moon Valley.

With these developments, Dad's vision had finally won the day.

When Dad recruited me, I was sitting in his car. He had a cigarette in his mouth and a silver Motorola flip phone in his hand.

"Son, the day someone can get care through this, it changes everything. And that day is coming."

I'll never forget the look on his face as he held that basic flip phone and forecasted an entire industry before the technological capability ever existed. He told me that if I could be the first to do it, I'd do extremely well.

He was right again.

Heading into the end of 2019, we were in a real position to thrive. We had nine facilities, all using integrated care and all using telehealth on our own, customized technology. From not even cracking the top fifty medical providers in the state, we were now in the top five privately owned medical groups and leading both telemedicine and integrated care.

Everything was going our way—just as COVID-19 reared its head on the other side of the ocean and threatened to upend everything.

9

HALT AND CATCH FIRE

Jamil gave birth to our twin daughters, Justice and Joy, on May 29, 2019. Joy, the youngest, was placed in the neonatal intensive care unit (NICU) for two weeks. Jamil never left her side. She brought Justice to the hospital with her to nurse while she sat with Joy. Jamil was being stretched thin. She was trying to care for three daughters and a husband all at once, all of us with different needs. It was more than any one person could do—especially after just giving birth.

Prior to the twins being born, I went on paternity leave and moved us into a new house while Jamil was on bed rest. When leave was over, I started working from my new home. Once the girls joined us, we barely left for the next six months. Basically, almost a year before the rest of the world, we were living in unofficial quarantine.

It was a time when I really came to embrace my role as a father of daughters. Spending all day in a household full of women, I became an even greater advocate for the importance of women taking leading roles across society. I've always taught my daughters to talk clearly and speak up because their voices need to be heard.

We managed to get back out into the world around Halloween 2019. Foolishly, we thought we were about to return to normal.

Justin, Jamil, Jurni, Justice and Joy
at Halloween (2019)

But there were already troubling signs of what was ahead. At the time, I was serving as a board member for the second-largest hospital system in Arizona, which I'd been asked to join in 2014. I brought a different perspective to these discussions, and I was there to help them improve outpatient services and think of strategies to keep patients who didn't need emergent care out of emergency rooms. Each month, I attended a three-hour-long board meeting and discussed the inner workings of hospitals and health plans with the other members.

In January 2020, I attended the meeting as I always did. There was a certain nervousness around the room. There were whispers about a new virus breaking out in China, but no one was making any plans to deal with it if—or when—it showed up in the US. At that moment, my thoughts stretched no further than my family. With young children in the house, the first priority for Jamil and me was keeping them healthy.

One month later, everything changed. We were in the February meeting when everyone's phones suddenly went off. The first case of COVID-19 had been discovered in Seattle.

The board's response shocked me. I don't know what I was expecting: immediate action, vigorous debate. It was nothing like that. No one knew what to do. The medical community hadn't been given any guidance from the CDC yet, and—locked in indecision—an atmosphere of nonchalance settled over the room. They had all seen these kinds of things pop up before, and usually it all fizzled out. Their plan was to wait for direction.

I wasn't satisfied with that. I was used to working with populations who had difficulty navigating systems, and I was worried that an outbreak would overwhelm everyone. I asked the question no one else seemed interested in addressing.

"What happens if this gets really serious?'

Shoulders shrugged around the room. "We'll keep an eye on it," someone said.

It was unsettling, but what else could they do? Their telehealth system wasn't set up; they didn't really have much more information than the general public. It seemed to me like a kind of paralysis. All they *could* do was wait.

But while they waited, things were quickly escalating.

A month later, I was on a flight to Orange County, California. My colleague and I were visiting a practice we were interested in acquiring. Everything seemed like business as usual—except that I was wearing a mask on the plane. It was only a day trip, but we had concerns over whether or not it was safe to travel.

By that time, the medical community was also paying closer attention to the unfolding situation. The March hospital board meeting was held over Zoom. But they still seemed to have as little clarity on the situation as everyone else in the country—and no large-scale plans to handle the outbreak had been put in place.

As my concern for the well-being of my growing family, my team at Bayless, and our thousands of patients grew, I began preparing as well as I could for what I now saw was inescapably coming. I started filling shopping carts with basic supplies. Other shoppers looked at me like I was crazy, but to me it was simple math. I was just anticipating the inevitable.

Early morning on March 13, 2020, when lockdowns were first announced, I was watching the news and worrying. Like every business owner, my initial thought was serious concern. Was my business going to fail just as I'd finally proved out our big vision? After so much struggle and sacrifice, was this the beginning of the end?

I rallied enough to run our weekly 8:00 a.m. meeting. That morning, we made the call to shut in-person services down and limit exposure at our administrative sites.

A lot of people thought I was overreacting. At that point, some of our administration team was still treating the situation as if it was nothing to worry about—a temporary inconvenience sure to end shortly—but it was clear to me that continued, full-capacity operations were unsustainable. The majority of our patients were part of at-risk groups. They were children and elderly. They had comorbidities and mental health issues. What if one of them got sick visiting us? We couldn't let that happen. So we sent everyone home. Within forty hours, every brick-and-mortar location would be closed.

I knew it was the right call to make, but shutting everything down still left me feeling incredibly low. To shake off my mood, I went to take a shower.

And there, I had an epiphany.

I realized that this wasn't the end of Bayless—it was an opportunity to reach our true potential. Back in '08, Carla Harris taught me "chaos brings opportunity" and "never let a good crisis go to waste." I certainly wasn't going to now.

I called an emergency meeting over Zoom.

"This is exactly what we've been waiting for," I told my staff. "This is our opportunity to shine. And our common rallying enemy will be COVID-19."

The Opportunity

Nothing could prove the power of telemedicine like a pandemic. It created a huge shift in momentum—just the motivation the last couple of holdouts needed to implement telehealth across our whole organization. Nothing would convince reticent patients to give the system a try like a lockdown. Nothing would push us to execute on our new system like the absence of a safety net.

To do this right, though, we'd have to set the company up to succeed.

With our offices shut, we ordered hundreds of laptops and a ton of N95 masks. We put HEPA filter fans and heat systems to scan faces and check for fever throughout our locations, then created new policies and procedures for entering the buildings. I instructed my team to begin recruiting more clinicians and getting our marketing in line so the community would know we were open and we offered telehealth at scale for the mind and body.

For two weeks, while we transitioned, our patient volume declined significantly.

We'd built the virtual platform, and we'd hired and trained a lot of people—but it still took time to transition systems and outreach existing patients. It took time for marketing to get the word out. We also had to train thousands of people on the system usage and how to be efficient on telemedicine across generational divides. So many people were anxious and sitting at home. I knew they were perfect potential clients; we just had to have a sense of urgency getting them on the system for the first time. I knew that once we got them on the platform, they would mostly be satisfied and prefer virtual over in-office—especially during a respiratory pandemic!

In the meantime, I held onto my blind faith that our system would prove sustainable—and refused to lay anyone off. We applied for PPP to cover our expenses over that period and paid for everything in the meantime through our savings.

By the time we got the check in the mail, we were up and running—and we never slowed down.

Helping People Heal

As we refined our pandemic response and started delivering telemedicine, widespread social unrest after George Floyd's death began driving even more members of our community to seek mental healthcare. Amid the riots, protests, and the contested police response—all of it rife with overt racial overtones—I recognized the need for a forum to help people understand and process the angst, frustration, and sadness the situation brought on.

I joined Jamil in praying for empathy, growth, and understanding in the world, but I also decided to take some concrete steps to do my part and join the conversation. I began by writing an email in which I revealed my own history with racial profiling. I told my entire network about getting pulled over by the police when I was a teenager and having a gun held to my head. I offered my story as a perspective to those who didn't understand why people were hurting, or who might have held certain beliefs about George Floyd. I wanted to explain why the event was so important and why it was causing so many problems. When it came to the police response, I remained carefully in the middle. I was very clear that I did not believe all police were bad, but I also highlighted that what happened was a more common problem than a lot of people realized—and that it had happened to someone they knew.

I also emphasized that pretending the problem didn't exist was part of the problem.

I sent the email out to my entire company, and I invited others to share their own stories. It was a way to provide support for our people, and we gradually worked through the hurt and confusion—together.

It was still tough. Looting had gotten out of control, and a mall in Scottsdale was broken into and practically destroyed. Things escalated to such a fever pitch that Jamil and I worried people would come and loot the neighborhood. One night, I stayed up until sunrise with a pistol in my hand.

Luckily, the violence never reached our home, and as tensions began to cool slightly, I was able to return my focus to the company and the services we were providing the community.

The Struggle of Building Structure

Every other practice in Phoenix had closed down at the beginning of lockdown. Once they were back up and running, they suddenly realized they'd been caught out by circumstances again. This time, it wasn't integrated care, it was the desperate need for telehealth technology. While they were scrambling, our growth was accelerating. By May, we saw greater week-over-week growth than we'd ever experienced before.

Everything began moving in the right direction. Our no-show rate plummeted, as our patients came not to just adapt to telemedicine but to really embrace it. Care improved, particularly for those populations that found it hardest to show up for every appointment. The unemployed, the disabled, those with low income and no transportation: suddenly, they were receiving a far higher level of care than they may have in their entire lives.

The momentum also reinforced a realization I'd had in 2018, when I found out Jamil was pregnant with the twins. I needed a full-time COO to run the company's day-to-day operations—someone who would supplement my skills and vision and scale the underlying practice.

This was a problem that had plagued me since I first realized it existed. Back in 2018, I started working with recruiting firms to find that specialized fit. In particular, I was looking for someone with a bit more experience. What I failed to consider was that no one had ever done what we were doing. We were building a brand-new model, and that made it difficult to find someone with the *right* experience.

Eventually, we hired someone. She had worked for many years in hospital systems and had a great resume for scaling practices. But there was a problem. As a rule, hospitals don't make money. They're funded through a mechanism that allows them to lose money on outpatient-ambulatory operations while making their profits through inpatient procedures.

That system wouldn't work in a business with an outpatient entrepreneurial engine. Additionally, this person didn't really fit our culture. She was older and used to hierarchies with strong support systems that didn't require placing an emphasis on profit. She wasn't well suited for a scrappy startup with departments with high levels of independence.

By July 2019, as we were opening new facilities, it became apparent that the new COO was not growing into her role. We hit a brick wall, and I ultimately had to remove her from her position and begin the search again.

In December of that year, I made the same mistake again when I hired a second COO. That person didn't work out either, and I let him go in April 2020.

I simply couldn't seem to find a partner who could take some of the responsibility off my shoulders and help me grow the company. I was beginning to feel burned out—just as the company was truly taking off. I started thinking a COO was the wrong play here. I needed something else. I might need a strategic partner.

Creating Systems of Support

In addition to navigating a pandemic, explosive growth, and the ups and downs of two unsuccessful COOs, there was also a lot to handle at home. We had three young kids in the house, and Jamil was having a hard time. She'd been a true believer in this project from the beginning, and she'd made innumerable sacrifices along the way. She'd already had to put off her career as a nurse practitioner for far too long. For long stretches, she was watching one and then three children on her own while I was working long days every day to make Bayless a success.

This was one of the downsides of my career. The sacrifice I'd been willing to make for myself in order to see the business succeed also meant my family had to sacrifice as well. In entrepreneurship, you are never the only one making the tough choices. Your family makes them with you, and Jamil had cosigned those choices all along the way with me. Now we were stuck in the house again—after we'd already spent most of the previous year locked inside—and it had finally become too much.

This would have been difficult enough, but we were also dealing with grief. In February, Craig's wife, Esther, had died after a long illness—the same one we'd had hints of back in Spain when she'd suddenly get fatigued. She had been an important part of our lives and losing her right before entering a global pandemic had been particularly hard on Jamil.

In April 2020, my mother-in-law, Debbie, flew down to visit. After seeing the state we were in, she decided to move in to help the family. Debbie gave the whole family an immediate boost. She took the pressure off Jamil and helped create a wonderful environment in our home. Because of her, we had a "good" pandemic—full of backyard barbecues and joyful family memories.

Debbie was also a support for me. She's an entrepreneur, so she understood the pressure I was under. And her stabilizing presence also allowed me to focus on supporting my team.

I worked with Michael Zistatsis, a friend who owned an Italian and Mediterranean restaurant—Alexi's Grill, Dad's old favorite spot—to provide meals for the team and their families while also supporting the restaurant. Like many restaurants, he'd shut down temporarily when the lockdowns were announced. I asked if there was a way I could get him to cater for my team, many of whom were having a harder time at home than I was. Michael worked a miracle and set up a system that allowed my team members to take home meals for their entire families. Michael told me afterward it helped him keep the lights on.

We contracted with another organization to give everyone mental health services. We worked with the Boys & Girls Club—who were following similar COVID-19 policies and protocols to our own—to give our people a place to send their kids during workdays. Childcare had become a huge issue for people, but we were able to meet that need at no charge to our team. It was a painful time for a lot of people, but we did everything we could to help.

Once we'd introduced our support system, we started opening our locations one day a week, doing everything we could to avoid a massive spread of the virus. We rotated which location was open each day and limited appointments to urgent and primary care only, thus creating access points across Phoenix. Eventually, we were able to open pediatrics two days a week. We ran a skeleton crew and followed strict procedures. Patients were prescreened over the phone before coming in and on-site. And our team was tested and cleared daily. We knew people would get COVID from family and friends, but our aim was to prevent COVID from entering and taking down an entire office.

To further reduce risk, we developed a zero-tolerance COVID policy. We didn't tell anyone they couldn't go to a restaurant or to a concert, but if they did that and didn't follow guidelines, they wouldn't work for Bayless anymore. We also mandated vaccination once it became available. We felt we had an obligation to our patients, first and foremost, and to our staff members. Besides the obvious dangers, a large outbreak would affect our business and, therefore, our ability to provide care.

It cost us a few people, but the vast majority stuck with us through it all.

The Definition of Success

Every decision we made throughout my tenure was run through three considerations: it had to be good for the business, good for the patient, and good for the staff.

This framing served us well.

Over the course of that COVID-19 year, while most organizations laid off people and struggled, we doubled our staff and the number of patients we saw. We hit record profits. At the same time, we had zero outbreaks. We never had a whole office get sick. And we proved our telehealth system could work on a massive scale.

Everyone at Bayless won over that period. We gave each person who stuck with us through the whole year additional compensation and had record take-home pay. We covered their mental health needs and fed their families.

In the end, we served the business, our people, and our patients as well as anyone in the medical world.

It was an incredible achievement, but I was still running on fumes. As we came out of the crisis in a far better position than when we entered it, I turned my attention back to our organizational needs. It was time I found that strategic partner.

10

FULL CIRCLE

By May 2020, we could see our strategies paying off.

Our marketing was everywhere. We flooded Pandora and social media—every resource people were using while they were stuck at home—to tell them they weren't alone. We acknowledged the rampant fear and anxiety the pandemic had caused and focused our message on how difficult it was to be stuck at home, taking care of the kids, working, and likely dealing with relationship issues they'd never experienced before. On top of everything, they might be ill. They might have COVID.

We told them we could help.

The message was clear: we could simultaneously address our patients' mental, emotional, and physical needs—even in the midst of lockdown.

As we started seeing massive growth, I went back to my business training. This was the time to monetize and seek even bigger growth. Most practices were struggling to make payroll, but ours was strong—and it had been for a few years now.

I felt confident it was time to look for that strategic partner I'd been considering—time to take some chips off the table so we could continue to grow and build.

To gain that advantage, I was open to selling part of the company. I hadn't settled on a percentage or particular structure—I just wanted it to be the right choice for our people. More important than ensuring a majority or minority sale was that we align with someone who shared our priorities but also had national scale. Bayless had become a very large small business, and we needed a partner who could turn us into a national entity.

We'd been telling people for years that this was the future. Now that we'd finally arrived at that future, it was time to test the market. We just needed someone who shared our vision so we could grow even further.

So of course, I called Carla.

By that time, Carla had become Morgan Stanley's vice chairwoman of Wealth Management. We chatted for a moment about how we'd each fared through the pandemic as I built up to my pitch.

"This is a call I've been waiting to make for a long time," I said.

I told her that I'd had some interest from potential buyers in the last couple years. I now thought Bayless was ready to take on a strategic partner and capitalize on our growth.

"Oh, you think you're ready?" she asked. "Then send over your stuff, and I'll show it to the investment banking division."

When her email response came, I couldn't help but smile. *Oh yeah*, it read. *You're ready*.

Normally, Morgan Stanley wouldn't fully take on a company of our size. We weren't *that* big. But our growth was impressive, and in that COVID-19 market, there weren't many deals being made. My previous relationship with Carla tipped the scales in our favor. She knew the company was heading in the right direction, and above all, she trusted my judgment. When I called my shot, I always hit it—nothing but net. Once Carla put her name behind the numbers, the bank was willing to take us on as a client.

We signed an engagement letter with them. Then we had to restructure the company—again.

I was ready for this. Our first restructure had taken place in 2010, when Dad was in the hospital and I transitioned Bayless & Associates from a PC to an incorporation. This time, we were transitioning to an LLC. That would give us the ability to sell units of the company in a tax benefit to the buyer.

Thanks to Carla, we were one step closer to finding that strategic partner.

Nine Figures

Morgan Stanley assigned us to an M&A banker named David Cohen. Before we could go to market in July, David and his team required a full review of our business.

They performed a quality of earnings audit to determine the true value of our revenue. Revenue is not all judged the same in a sale. For instance, our PPP loan wasn't considered earnings—it was a one-time influx of cash that happened as a result of extraordinary circumstances. In essence, Morgan Stanley combed through our history of revenue to make sure our earnings were actually what we said they were. It was like a colonoscopy for the business.

This intense, comprehensive financial exam went on for three months. They asked questions going back years. Fortunately, I had Angie, who was still my controller and CPA. Her excellent recordkeeping and our overall preparedness carried the day.

Although an audit of that magnitude is typically as unpleasant as it sounds, it was actually done for our own benefit. Knowing precisely what our earnings were put us in a position of strength when we presented our materials to potential buyers on the road show—the series of presentations we'd make to potential buyers. It gave us ammunition for any who doubted our numbers. When we told them what the company was worth, we were certain, and we could back it up.

David Cohen and I put together a brilliant pitch book for the road show that explained who we were and what we did. He had all potential buyers in place by Labor Day 2020.

And then the virtual road show began.

We met with middle-market private equity firms, blue-chip private equity firms, and strategics—competitors or ancillary providers who wanted the capabilities we had.

Then one day, I got a call from a chief medical officer at the first RBHA company that had shot down my ideas all those years ago. I'd known her for many years. She'd been a real believer in our ideas long before we'd proven them out, so I was more open to her than I might have been with others at her organization.

"We've been watching you guys grow," she said. "Would you be interested in having a conversation?"

I informed her we were doing a road show and invited her company to come along.

All in all, I met with around fifty companies and pitched them between Labor Day and Halloween—while still running the business full time. Around Halloween we started asking for letters of intent from interested firms—in other words, actual bids.

At that point, I had no idea how much we were actually worth. Last time someone had offered to buy us, it was a local company that was backed by a private equity company in 2017. They'd offered us around $15 million—but ultimately, we walked away because of culture and fit. I knew we were bigger than that now. But how much bigger?

Much.

We started getting several very real, tangible bids in the mid-eight- and low-nine-figure range. It gave us a lot to consider. The details varied widely between these bids—each one offering different terms on the size of the stake being sold, my position going forward, and how they saw the businesses working together and expanding into new markets differently.

Most importantly for me, I needed to be certain that the people making these bids would be a good partner. Did they really get what we were about? Did they believe in scaling our vision? Would they really do what they claimed they were going to do?

When I talked to Kyle, he echoed this point. It was less about the figure than whether this company could partner with me to take Bayless national.

"If they're serious about that," he said, "you should take their offer."

In the end, things came full circle. We decided to go with our one-time rival, the former RBHA company. They bought a 70 percent stake for a mid-nine-figure valuation. We finished negotiating terms on December 2 and closed four days before Christmas.

All the years I spent fighting and being laughed at had—*finally*—paid off. As Jamil noted at the time, this was bigger than a big payday. It was the end of a journey, and the start of another. Dad's dreams and mine were fully realized, and the company was poised to reach new markets, new patients, and new heights.

What to Do When the Music Stops

I was confident I'd made the right call in selling Bayless. It was an extremely difficult decision, but I knew that selling would allow the company to accelerate its vision and operational support. With more investment, we could benefit from being an early mover in integrated care and telemedicine, scaling while everyone else was still catching up.

The market dynamics were right, and I couldn't just ignore that. Timing is everything in entrepreneurship. Go too early or too late, and you can miss your window of opportunity, no matter how good your product or service. The window of opportunity created by COVID-19 wouldn't last forever.

Additionally, I had a young family—one that I'd spent far too much time away from. I was tired of putting them second while I chased my dream. Selling offered me the chance to monetize the work I'd done to date, while giving me the time to be with the people I loved most.

So, as I say, I was content with my choice—but that didn't make the transition out of the business any easier. No one ever prepares you for the moment the music stops. You spend years climbing and climbing with your business, digging deeper and deeper to reach the summit in your industry. Selling your company is the moment of ultimate triumph—the chance to finally take the chip off your shoulder and show that you had what it takes—but no one talks about what happens after.

What do you do the next day, when no one calls and no one emails? What do you do when there's no office to go into anymore and no one asking for your advice on how to run things? For the first time in years, you can sit still, but you don't know how to do anything but run anymore.

For that reason, transitioning out of Bayless was one of the hardest things I've ever done. It's no exaggeration to say it took almost as much of a toll as losing Dad.

The only way through was to decide on a direction for the next journey. I had to give myself a project that made me get up in the morning. I had to pick a new mountain to climb.

That's what I did. I turned my focus in a new direction. I decided it was time to put my energy into giving back.

Go Back and Give Back

I've always believed in giving back, and I started doing so long before selling the company. In my early years at Bayless, when I'd first returned to Phoenix, I reached out to a former teacher from my Catholic high school—the one who had profiled me and then later apologized. I didn't have large sums of money to donate at that point, but I wanted to give back by teaching kids about entrepreneurship. She heartily agreed and championed my idea. By then, she was the principal and in a position to create a position for me. For years, I taught a curriculum for juniors and seniors who were interested in business and gave them an option to eventually intern at Bayless.

I also taught at GateWay Community College, working with kids who already had an interest in business and had taken electives in economics or finance during high school. In my class, they learned how to put together a basic business plan, and then they all pitched to my executive team. The winners of the pitch would get an interview for a summer internship and a prize (usually gold or silver coins to show the value of investment and teach them about commodities). My executive assistant for three years came from this program.

As soon as the deal with the strategic partner was done, I knew I could make an even bigger impact. My first call was to Morehouse. In the climate of examining social injustice in our society that emerged during the pandemic, I felt compelled to help young people learn about wealth creation and the power of larger-scale entrepreneurship in disadvantaged communities. A big part of the problem in those communities is that there's no real road map to create wealth outside of professional sports, entertainment, or working within the structure of someone else's corporation. Bayless had just proven the power of entrepreneurship, and I wanted to make sure the next generation knew there was an alternative path available to them.

So I reached out to Professor Onifade and told him I wanted to make a major contribution that focused on creating a program in entrepreneurship. Morehouse was founded in 1867 but up to that time still had no real entrepreneurship training or curriculum. There were very few programs that taught around it, but no actual degree program. Instead, the business training prepared students to join big corporations, just as I had joined Morgan Stanley. I wanted to repay the Presidential Scholarship I'd been given so the next generation of entrepreneurs could leave school without debt and take bigger entrepreneurial shots.

Justin and Morehouse Scholarship Recipients

My second call was to the Boys & Girls Club. They'd been a partner with us at Bayless for many years. Because of them, we could give our team childcare during the pandemic. Before that, they'd given me a place to go when I was a kid. If not for them, I wouldn't have been able to keep playing basketball. I wanted to pay back those opportunities, and I also wanted to make sure the kids going there now had a better understanding of business. I partnered with them to create a program that helped kids with that.

Jill Johnson, Jamil and Justin at Boys & Girls Club
Entrepreneurship Program Announcement

Then I called my old Catholic high school again. I'd long ago stopped teaching there, but I still wanted to support the school. So I donated to scholarships for disadvantaged students through Catholic Education Arizona. That way, more kids like me could go to a great school and have the education to do great things in the future.

In essence, what I was able to do at Morehouse, the Boys & Girls Club, and my high school was formalize programs that built on my ideas from teaching. Schools typically teach people to be good employees—but not how to start and grow their own business. I wanted to change all that.

I told everyone I helped that all I asked in return was that when they found themselves in a position to pay it forward, they'd provide the same opportunity to the next generation. I didn't want to hear about anyone pulling the ladder up after them. I wanted each of them adding ladders for the next ones in line to climb up.

My aim was to create a hundred more of me, helping a hundred times the kids I helped with my contributions. And if each one of that hundred helped even a fraction more—we could change everything.

The Journey to Ten Figures

So, what's next?

My focus now is continuing on the path I've set since the sale of the company. The question is how to take these initiatives even further. How do we help future dark horse entrepreneurs live up to their potential?

In its way, the world of professional sports knows exactly how to do that. Over the years, I've watched the systems created to farm talent within that industry. If you're a talented athlete and you're young, there's a certain point at which people will realize you're not just good—you're good enough to go all the way.

What happens next depends on the sport, but every sport has a system in place to build that talent and funnel it toward the big leagues. In baseball, often by high school, you've got an offer to play in the A, AA, or AAA league and develop your talent right away. The NBA has the G League, and the NHL has overseas leagues. Jerryd went to the Amateur Athletic Union to sharpen his skills, and then to the University of Arizona—which was a great school for his position, point guard. He was being brought up to go to the pros.

We've long had these mechanisms of support in place for athletes, but there aren't any leagues for entrepreneurs with talent—particularly those who come from communities without a lot of connections further up the economic chain. Their only option is to get into a good school and then usually go work for a big corporation, which requires a different skill set and doesn't help develop their entrepreneurial talent. Otherwise, they have to take a huge risk and figure the whole process out for themselves.

My mission now is to change these circumstances by creating a funnel that allows young entrepreneurs to develop their talents—the same way baseball scouts go to communities to bring young talent through the ranks and up to the pros.

My goal here is ambitious—perhaps as ambitious as taking on the State of Arizona and changing the medical system. I want to create an entire minor league system for entrepreneurs and eliminate the social determinants of entrepreneurship. Such a league would give young adults access to the tools that will facilitate their entrepreneurial development by supporting their cost of living, caring for their mental health (through performance coaching), and providing mentorship to help them spin out business ideas in the medical sphere—particularly the sort that can improve the lives of people in their community.

Basically, I want to provide young entrepreneurs with everything they need to swing for the fences.

To do this, I'm developing three separate organizations. The first is The Journey Venture Studio. This not-for-profit, 501(c)(3) charitable organization is A-league ball for entrepreneurs in the healthcare space, primarily between the ages of eighteen and thirty-five. We aim to offer a small number of these young entrepreneurs the opportunity to spend eight months in Phoenix developing their ideas in six areas:

- mental health
- sports medicine
- women's health
- chronic disease management
- aging and elder care
- packaging and supply chain

Each entrepreneur will receive $110,000, covering all startup and personal expenses. Over that eight-month period, they'll also receive coaching and mentoring, as well as legal, marketing, branding, and technological support. This founder-in-residence program will give them the business skills ambitious leaders like my father never received—the tools necessary to change the world and build scalable healthcare venture-backed companies.

At the end of that eight months, they'll have the opportunity to pitch the vision for their startup to a team of investors for their pre-seed fundraising round. If the investors like what they see, The Journey will help them incorporate their new company and will serve as a cofounder, providing long-term guidance as the business establishes itself and scales.

One of the investors at the pitch will be my second project, Ten Figures. Ten Figures is the AA league: an early-stage venture capital firm specifically tasked with investing in disruptive startups with founders and customers from underrepresented communities. While investment won't be limited to graduates of The Journey, those graduates are a natural fit for Ten Figures investment.

At this point, we'll have taken entrepreneurial talent, helped them found and incorporate a business, and provided initial investment to get those ideas off the ground. The last stage in the funnel is getting the kind of investment I needed to take Bayless national. This is AAA stuff—the last stage of development before you really hit the pros. And this is where Carla and Morgan Stanley come back in.

As my idea for The Journey and Ten Figures took shape, I reached out to Carla once more. She asked me to come spend some time with her in New York. We played some golf while I ran through the details, and she made me an offer: to join a new institutional venture capital fund at Morgan Stanley focused on minority founders in different early-stage verticals, called Morgan Stanley Next Level Fund. She'd assembled a team with a unique set of "superpowers," with each member capable of mentoring entrepreneurs in a particular industry. She recruited Microsoft as the board's technology champion, Walmart as the consumer retail champion, and Hearst Labs as the media entertainment champion. Morgan Stanley would handle everything in FinTech.

When we spoke, she was still looking for one final member: a healthcare champion. And she felt I fit the bill.

Carla offered me a seat on the limited partner advisory board, and I signed the deal in August 2022. I started my career with Morgan Stanley as a banker. It's where I learned the value of an intense work ethic. I've always said that I didn't need an MBA because I got that education through the Morgan Stanley boot camp. They also helped me find a strategic partner and transition through selling my company into this focus. And now I'm helping them as the only entrepreneur involved with their venture capital fund to identify who to invest in in the future.

Justin and Carla Harris

Talk about going full circle. With Morgan Stanley as a partner, entrepreneurs will now have a clear path through the minor leagues to the entrepreneurial pros. There's a place they can go to develop their ideas, a place to go to get initial startup funding, and a place to go when they're ready to see their early success scale.

These three projects will allow me to invest in the next generation of great dark horse entrepreneurs—and to find the ones who can outdo me and reach a ten-figure valuation.

And I hope one of them is you.

CONCLUSION

Reviewing my life and the success I've experienced, I sometimes wonder why it is that I was the one who saw a better path forward in mental health for Arizona. The state is filled with smart, dedicated people who would like to provide those services. Why was I the one who saw a better way forward?

In writing this book, I believe I have discovered the answer. I created that solution precisely because of the life I've lived. I was born into a family of hustlers with business acumen and entrepreneurial ambitions. I was an outsider who saw things differently and never quite fit in anywhere. I had incredible mentors, a natural gift for mathematics, and a chip on my shoulder that motivated me to take on any odds in my journey to success.

I don't think I could have done what I did without those qualities. In other words, I didn't look like the traditional CEO of a mental health company, and that is what made the difference.

In that space, at the time, every company was run by clinicians who had gone back to school for some business training. Almost everyone at the top of those organizations was White. They came up through that system and took it for granted. They couldn't see it with clear eyes, particularly when they were profiting from business as usual.

In many ways, I was their exact opposite—the dark horse that most people dismissed as the wrong fit for the industry. I was Black, young, and trained primarily in business. I was running a business, not a nonprofit. I had concerns and responsibilities that they didn't. I had to make Bayless profitable, and I couldn't just get more grants to make up for shortfalls.

But it was that outsider perspective that allowed me to see a way through all the broken bureaucracy. I was part of the community being underserved, so I couldn't just shrug about it. I was young, new, and trained with a business eye to solve problems. That allowed me to see where the system was letting us down. It allowed me to streamline administrative functions and buy time while we proved out integrated care.

All of which is to say, my life, my family, my mentors, and numerous sacrifices made my success possible. And I believe that's always the case for entrepreneurs. Much of what you might see as limitations in your own experience can prove your greatest assets. The discrimination I faced, the breaking up of my family, the sacrifices and the setbacks—those are the circumstances that made me the person capable of my success.

I'm sure the same is true of you. Being a dark horse is an asset. Having to take the harder road is a benefit. These circumstances give you the opportunity to see the problems and the solutions better than anyone who had an easier way into the industry you're targeting.

You have everything it takes for success. All you have to do is go out and prove it.

I truly believe you can be a dark horse success just like me. That's why I wrote this book. And it's why I've created The Journey Venture Studio and Ten Figures, and joined the Morgan Stanley Next Level Fund. Combining these opportunities with your innate entrepreneurial talents, we could achieve incredible things.

The path to success is not easy. As we've seen in this book, it often means you will be laughed at and dismissed. It may mean you are held back by corrupt, broken systems that prejudge you. At some point, you will be desperate and tired. This path will require sacrifice and grit. But if you have the skills, vision, and ambition of an entrepreneur—and someone willing to give you a chance—*you* can change the world.

The odds remain stacked against us, but together, I believe we can change those odds. These are the times great companies and founders are made. Pressure always makes diamonds. So reach out to The Journey Venture Studio, Ten Figures, or the Morgan Stanley Next Level Fund so we can go on this journey together.

I can't wait to see what dark horse ideas you'll show me.

APPENDIX I

I'm often asked for advice on becoming an entrepreneur. To live up to your entrepreneurial potential, I've assembled ten recommendations—the keys I've discovered in reviewing my own journey:

1. **Never be afraid to blaze your own trail.** Coming back to take over my father's business was never the obvious play for me. Taking on the Medicaid system, championing an integrated care model that few believed in, and keeping the faith in telemedicine: Those were decisions way off the standard path. But without those decisions, I would never have reached this level of success.
2. **Those closest to you will often cause the most pain and are sometimes the biggest doubters—always trust your gut.** Nothing was harder for me than the times when my father didn't believe in my vision. It was always difficult to come up against friends, family, and colleagues when they had doubts about my choices. It took a lot of internal strength to forge ahead anyway. The path to success is often a lonely one, and those closest to you can often be the largest source of doubt.
3. **Get comfortable with the uncomfortable. Learn to enjoy the feeling of discomfort and realize this**

is needed for growth and transformation. I spent months driving the Green Bomber while I went without a salary. There were times I definitely had to fake it like I made it while I was barely holding on. I ended up in rooms where I felt like the odd man out every time. But every time, I went back. Those periods strengthened me and gave me the skills I needed to succeed further down the line.

4. **Establish routines for work, family, and health. These are nonnegotiables that will keep you focused and able to withstand the mental, physical, and emotional journey ahead.** I couldn't have achieved what I did before and during COVID-19 if I didn't have routines in place that would give me time with Jamil and my daughters. Taking vacations, like the one we took with Craig and Esther in Spain, can rejuvenate you, inspire you, and allow you to double your efforts when you get back. You must prepare your body and mind before going through intense periods of struggle in your business—just as an athlete would prepare for a marathon.
5. **When you make your first million, don't let it go to your head. Reinvest first in your future and your family.** I get asked often what I did with my first "check." I bought a universal whole life policy for my family, paid off my house . . . and then I bought a new car. When I sold Bayless, my first thought was how I could give back to others instead of how I could further benefit myself. Earning that big payday is part of the reason people become entrepreneurs, but you should balance the fun with responsible finances and giving back to others.
6. **Find something to motivate you tangibly along the journey.** A mentor of mine once suggested I buy

a watch for every win or milestone. It doesn't have to be a watch, but you do need some way to celebrate success and effort. It is a reminder that the next time you are going through the struggle, you can figure out a way to conquer the barrier and become better. If you are interested in watches, I highly suggest you spend time reading about high horology and specifically my favorite brand: Audemars Piguet. You will quickly understand why they are my favorite.

7. **Not all attorneys are made equal and as talented as others.** It goes against the entrepreneurial instinct, but with lawyers, it's always best to hire the best for the transaction instead of seeking the best deal. Identify the best attorneys and pay them their full fees. You will be glad you did. Trust me, many of my own setbacks in this process came from hiring the wrong lawyers.
8. **Never take advice from someone who hasn't done it themself.** There are people in my life who thought I could never do what I did. They told me to get into sports marketing. They told me to play it safe and stick with a corporate job. But that advice usually came from the outside, from people who had never run a company or taken on such ambitious goals. They meant well, but their advice was best ignored.
9. **Be prepared for the weirdest breakup of your life after you sell your company.** Leaving Bayless was surreal. The rules were that there could be no emails or communication after I transitioned out. I left with a feeling of accomplishment but also a new emptiness. The project I'd dedicated my life to was over. You have to be prepared for the day the music stops.
10. **Always be true to yourself and unapologetic about your nature.** My best friend, Kyle, is the kind of person who can command a room at will. I can hold

> an audience, but it isn't my natural talent. I'm better one-on-one. I have a good sense of when someone is worth investing my time in, and I'm strong on those individual relationships. I'm also smart but stubborn. I can be idealistic, and I can keep a chip on my shoulder. It was this particular mix of characteristics that made my success possible. You don't have to change who you are; you have to make who you are work for what you're trying to accomplish.

These are not the only lessons you can take from my life or this book, but they're a good start to help you on your way. Good luck.

APPENDIX 2

Text of the full email sent upon my resigning at Morgan Stanley:

Good morning!
Family, Friends, and Colleagues,
Today, May 30, 2008, is my last day at Morgan Stanley.

First, thank you for everyone's support in my journey, but my stint in Corporate America has come to its rightful end.

Several of you have asked what my plans are going forward and how I could abandon Wall Street and the path I'm currently on with a great company, team, city, and learning opportunity. I have debated now for months and have come to a simple answer: history says it is time.

Eighty-seven years ago to the day, June 1, 1921, marks the anniversary of "BLACK WALL STREET," the name fittingly given to one of the most affluent all-BLACK communities in America, when it was bombed from the air and burned to the ground by mobs of envious whites. In a period spanning fewer than twelve hours, a once-thriving Black business district in northern Tulsa, Oklahoma, lay smoldering—a model community destroyed and a major African American economic movement resoundingly defused.

The night's carnage left some three thousand African Americans dead and over six hundred successful businesses lost. Among these were twenty-one churches, twenty-one restaurants, thirty grocery stores and two movie theaters, plus a hospital, a bank, a post office, libraries, schools, law offices, a half dozen private airplanes and even a bus system. As could have been expected, the impetus behind it all was the infamous Ku Klux Klan, working in consortia with ranking city officials and many other sympathizers.

The best description of BLACK WALL STREET, or Little Africa as it was also known, would be to compare it to a mini Beverly Hills. It was the golden door of the BLACK community during the early 1900s, and it proved that African Americans could create a successful infrastructure. That's what BLACK WALL STREET was all about.

The dollar circulated thirty-six to one hundred times, sometimes taking a year for currency to leave the community. Now a dollar leaves the BLACK community in fifteen minutes. As far as resources, there were PhDs residing in Little Africa, BLACK attorneys and doctors. One doctor was Dr. Berry who owned the bus system. His average income was $500 a day, a hefty pocket change in 1910.

It was a time when the entire state of Oklahoma had only two airports, yet six BLACKS owned their own planes. It was a very fascinating community. The mainstay of the community was to educate every child. Nepotism was the one word they believed in.

BLACK WALL STREET was a prime example of the typical, BLACK community in America that did businesses, but it was in an unusual location. You see, at the time, Oklahoma was set aside to be a BLACK and Indian state. There were over twenty-eight BLACK townships there. One-third of the people who traveled in the terrifying "Trail of Tears" alongside the Indians between 1830 and 1842 were BLACK people.

The citizens of this proposed Indian and BLACK state chose a BLACK governor; a treasurer from Kansas named McDade.

But the Ku Klux Klan said that if he assumed office that they would kill him within forty-eight hours. A lot of BLACKS owned farmland, and many of them had gone into the OIL business. The community was so tight and wealthy because they traded dollars hand-to-hand, and because they were dependent upon one another as a result of the Jim Crow laws.

It was not unusual that if a resident's home accidentally burned down, it could be rebuilt within a few weeks by neighbors. This was the type of scenario that was going on day-to-day on BLACK WALL STREET. When Blacks intermarried into the Indian culture, some of them received their promised "40 acres and a mule," and with that came whatever OIL was later found on the properties.

On BLACK WALL STREET, a lot of global business was conducted, and the community flourished from the early 1900s until June 1, 1921. That's when the largest massacre of nonmilitary Americans in the history of this country took place, and it was led by the KU KLUX KLAN. Imagine walking out of your front door and seeing 1,500 homes being burned.

It cost the BLACK community everything, and not a single dime of restitution—no insurance claims—has been awarded the victims to this day. Nonetheless, they rebuilt. It is estimated that 1,500 to 3,000 people were killed, and we know that a lot of them were buried in mass graves all around the city.

So where does this brief history lesson leave us today? What has been built since the destruction to replicate BLACK WALL STREET?

Many of my close friends and classmates have been regarded as some of the best and brightest minds in Black America, yet almost all of us ended up captivated by the lures and supposed wealth that one could achieve in Corporate America (and we have even dared to call ourselves Black Wall Street!).

While the opportunity to grow and develop under the corporate umbrella presents a premier and tremendous opportunity for most young Black college graduates, many become comfortable and remain idle within the construct for their entire career.

When do we completely change this mold? When do we all say it is enough and begin to grow our own businesses for our communities? When is it our time to each branch out and do our own Obama and completely turn the world upside down?

I am one who believes in everything happening for a reason and that we are each predetermined to fulfill a void in this world. The end of my journey is linked ironically with other family members, mentors, and colleagues' transformation into new positions and personal journeys.

As many of you know, I am moving back to Arizona, and I am proud that I will be working alongside my father at Bayless and Associates. This is where I plan to create change and build upon the vision my father set thirty years ago.

I also plan to work with my younger brother on strategic investments and relationships in his new career as a professional basketball player. Right now, he is currently projected to be drafted fourth to the Seattle Supersonics. For those who are not basketball fans, the Sonics are currently in court hearings to move to no other place than OKLAHOMA!

Ironic? Coincidence? Or maybe the correct word is OPPORTUNITY? Only time will tell for now.

In closing, I hope that many of you can see that our world is rapidly changing. History always repeats itself. When the "Black Wall Street" returns, my question is simple—are you one who plans to be instrumental in the change or are you one who is simply observant to the change?

My new contact information will follow this email later today.

Catch you on the street,
JB

ACKNOWLEDGMENTS

Life is short. Our time on this earth is relatively insignificant in the grand scheme of the universe. I don't know where I learned this (most likely my mother), but I have known since my teenage years that the only response to this fact is to truly find your purpose.

Finding and following purpose is no easy road. As the brilliant thinker and activist W.E.B. Du Bois said, "The most important thing to remember is this: to be ready at any moment to give up what you are for what you might become." The relentless pursuit of your purpose, without regard to what others believe, is the essence of an entrepreneur's journey.

It takes generations of sacrifice, years of staring into an unknown abyss, and a village of support for one individual to make this choice—especially when coming from any kind of disadvantaged background. Success cannot be viewed in a vacuum, as it is not solely the effort of one individual. My story of purpose and success is no different. And such a story necessitates deep gratitude.

I mention all this here in an effort to show just how intensely grateful I am for the people who have loved and supported me in my pursuit of purpose. I can't thank my mom, dad, and brother enough, nor Jamil, Jurni, Justice, and Joy. I don't have a story without you.

I feel similarly about my extended family—all the Bowman, Tubbs, Schwartz, Bowen, McCloud, and Bayless clans. I especially want to highlight my appreciation to Uncle Fred, Uncle Craig, Aunt Ila, Cousin Dennis, Cousin Michael, and Cousin Anika. I've always been able to rely on you for your history, your wisdom, and your love.

To all my friends and colleagues—Tyler, Kyle, Vince, Andrea W., Big Rich, Hillary, Jovanie, Andrea R., Burton, Hairat, Jon, Jill, Tom, Michael Z., Jim, Eddie, Roger, Dwayne, Arash, Valencia, Angie, Melissa, Aaron, Lynne, Lilach, Katie, Andy, Steve, Jason K., Kris, Jason W., Jason D., Tim, Marloin, Rob, Johnny, Derek, Rod, Wyatt, Reggie, Michael, Mark, Mario, Doug, Matt, Arnold, David, Mike—you have all had a huge impact on my life. I can't thank you enough for the good times, the tough times, the crazy times, and all your support throughout.

To all my mentors and teachers—including but not limited to Mrs. Payne, Mr. Stidham, Mr. Farrell, Mrs. Fessler, Mrs. Sanger, Coach Floco, Coach Lopez, Dr. Onifade, Dr. Hollingsworth, Dr. Allen, Dr. White, Mr. McLaurin, Michael Erath, and Dr. Pelberg—thank you for believing in me. That belief helped me dream the big dreams I've had and prepared me for the challenges I've encountered.

I want to especially thank Carla Harris. I hope to carry forward your incredible impact on so many people's lives. Thank you for believing in me early on and for all your continued support and guidance.

I would also like to thank all the current and former Bayless Healthcare, Ten Figures, and Journey Venture Studio team members, as well as anyone who I have had the opportunity to work, collaborate, or partner with through the years.

To Seth Libby and the entire publishing team for this book, even through the bankruptcy of the prior publisher, we were able to get this story across the finish line.

To the Greater Phoenix community, thank you for your support through all the years and for trusting my family with your healthcare needs. You're at the heart of my purpose. Your health is our legacy. None of this was possible without you.

ENDNOTES

1 National Center for Health Statistics, "Health, United States–Data Finder," mental health, Centers for Disease Control and Prevention, accessed February 28, 2024, https://www.cdc.gov/nchs/hus/data-finder.htm?&subject=Mental%20health.

2 American Psychological Association, "Psychologists Struggle to Meet Demand Amid Mental Health Crisis," practitioner survey, November 2022, https://www.apa.org/pubs/reports/practitioner/2022-covid-psychologist-workload.

3 Charlotte Huff, "Psychology's Diversity Problem," *Monitor on Psychology* 52, no. 7 (October 1, 2021): 45–51, https://www.apa.org/monitor/2021/10/feature-diversity-problem.

4 Mental Health America, "Ranking the States 2022," accessed February 28, 2024, https://mhanational.org/issues/2022/ranking-states#overall-ranking.

5 National Center for Health Statistics, "Health, United States–Data Finder."

Made in the USA
Las Vegas, NV
16 August 2024

93950512R00114